# Essential Guides for
# EARLY CAREER TEACHERS

# Teaching Early Years

# Essential Guides for Early Career Teachers

The *Essential Guides for Early Career Teachers* provide accessible, carefully researched, quick reads for early career teachers, covering the key topics you will encounter during your training year and first two years of teaching. They complement and are fully in line with the new Early Career Framework and are intended to assist ongoing professional development by bringing together current information and thinking on each area in one convenient place. The texts are edited by Emma Hollis, Executive Director of NASBTT (the National Association of School-Based Teacher Trainers), who brings a wealth of experience, expertise and knowledge to the series.

# Essential Guides for
# EARLY CAREER
# TEACHERS

# Teaching
# Early Years

Lorna Williams and Colin Howard
Series editor: Emma Hollis

Routledge
Taylor & Francis Group

LONDON AND NEW YORK

NASBTT

First published in 2022 by Critical Publishing Ltd

Published 2025 by Routledge
4 Park Square, Milton Park, Abingdon, Oxon OX14 4RN
605 Third Avenue, New York, NY 10017

*Routledge is an imprint of the Taylor & Francis Group, an informa business*

British Library Cataloguing in Publication Data
A CIP record for this book is available from the British Library

ISBN: 9781915080134 (pbk)
ISBN: 9781041055495 (ebk)

**Cartoon illustrations by Élisabeth Eudes-Pascal represented by GCI**
Figure artwork for Chapters 1 to 5 created by Glen Williams
Figure artwork for Chapter 6 created by Colin Howard

Cover and text design by Out of House Limited

DOI: 10.4324/9781041055495

# Dedication

*It takes a big heart to shape little minds.*

Unknown

This book is dedicated to all amazing early years teachers embarking on their early career journey who will inspire the next generation of little minds.

# Contents

# Meet the series editor

### Emma Hollis

I am Executive Director of NASBTT (the National Association of School-Based Teacher Trainers) and my absolute passion is teacher education. After gaining a first-class degree in psychology, I trained as a primary teacher, and soon became head of initial teacher training for a SCITT provider. I am dedicated to ensuring teachers are given access to high-quality professional development at the early stages of and throughout their careers.

# Meet the authors

### Lorna Williams

I am a senior lecturer on a primary teacher education team where I lead the early years and support and mentor future early years teachers. I am the PGCE early years cohort lead at the University of Worcester. I was an early years teacher in schools and a pre-school setting for almost 20 years. During my primary teaching career, I taught Years 1 and 2 in large infant schools and taught Reception and Year 1 in a village primary school. I have been involved in the opening of an on-site pre-school and enthusiastically embraced my role as an early years phase leader. I have always been passionate about the early years and each child's unique development and early learning journey.

## Colin Howard

I am an associate lecturer in initial teacher education at the University of Worcester. I have been involved in primary education for over 30 years and have been a successful headteacher in both small village and large primary settings. My research interests link to primary science, mentoring trainees, school leadership, SEND and teacher professional identity. I have written publications associated with primary science, teachers' and students' mental health and well-being, British Values, mentoring in schools and school leadership and management. I am dedicated to mentoring and supporting students to become outstanding teachers of the future.

# Foreword

As a passionate advocate of high-quality teacher education and continuing professional development (CPD), it had always been a source of frustration for me that, historically, beyond the ITT year, access to high-quality, structured ongoing professional development was always something of a lottery for teachers. Access to high-quality support was patchy, with some schools and local authorities offering fantastic opportunities for teachers throughout their careers while in other locations CPD was given lip service at best and, at worst, was non-existent.

This series was conceived to attempt to close some of those gaps and to offer accessible professional learning to busy teachers in the early stages of their careers. It was therefore a moment of genuine pleasure when the proposals for an entitlement for all early career teachers (ECTs) to receive a package of support, guidance and education first landed on my desk. Through the Early Career Framework, there is now a genuine opportunity for school communities to work together to offer the very best early career development for our most precious of resources – the teachers in our schools.

The aim of this series is to distil some of the key topics which occupy the thoughts of ECTs into digestible, informative texts which will promote discussion, contemplation and reflection and will spark further exploration into practice. In each edition, you will find a series of practical suggestions for how you can put the 'big idea' in each chapter into practice: now, next week and in the long term. By offering opportunities to bring the learning into the classroom in a very concrete way, we hope to help embed many of the principles we share into your day-to-day teaching.

This title is carefully crafted to support ECTs who are embarking on a career teaching in early years. It is also a must-read for all ECTs teaching in the primary phase as it gives such clear and important insights into those formative and crucial early experiences for children starting school for the first time. As a primary teacher, I wish I had been given the opportunity to read this title at the start of my career.

I hope you enjoy reading it as much as I have enjoyed editing it.

*Emma Hollis*
Executive Director, NASBTT

# Introduction

This book has been born out of a love for the early years and has been written by teaching professionals who are committed to early years initial teacher education (ITE). We believe early career teachers (ECTs) are the future for our children and for their educational success.

Having been through teacher training, where you have honed your craft, you will now start your journey as an early years ECT – a milestone in your life and without any shadow of doubt a great source of pride and excitement. You have listened and learnt from others and this will have allowed you to find your own unique voice. Like a magpie you will have collected 'pieces of gold' which you will have stored ready to share with your own class and setting. It is now time not only to have your own class but also to establish yourself in a wider team of teaching professionals. Yours will be a distinctive and significant voice which places the well-being and success of every unique child at their heart of your practice. You will provide the foundations of your pupils' future social, emotional and academic success. This will be driven by a passion to be outstanding, while wishing to embrace and drive forward change and improve teaching and learning wherever possible.

You will be part of a very special phase and key stage which can sometimes be forgotten by others. It is underpinned by a much-needed knowledge of child development and the Early Years Foundation Stage (EYFS) curriculum. You will need to be creative both within the classroom and when outdoors. This will allow you to keep your learning environment fresh and exciting and to stimulate children's curiosity. You will need to place early subject knowledge, effective planning and assessment at the centre of your practice to provide outstanding provision. This will inevitably involve a balance between focused activities and continuous provision activities. By placing the child at the core of their learning you will facilitate opportunities for children to develop their personal learning journey and make progress.

You will never be alone in your own teaching journey as long as you are able to foster effective relationships. As you work with the youngest pupils in the school, you will often be in the unique position of being a first point of contact for parents and carers regarding their child's new and exciting school journey – a position where there will be a focus on providing the building blocks of success. This will also involve early identification and intervention to support a child's future education. Relationships will be at the heart of your practice and will involve engaging parents and carers as partners, your other teaching colleagues, teaching assistants and other wider professional colleagues.

You will possess a unique skillset and knowledge which can be shared with others. Not only for the benefit of your school and pupils but also the wider partnership of similar colleagues in other settings. Your journey has just started and you will no doubt have a bright and long career in front of you. It may involve, after some time, a move to other schools and/or the establishment of a career journey with other additional curricular responsibilities and leadership roles. You will mould and shape your future with your own hopes and desires to become whatever you wish for yourself. Remember, like the children you teach, you too are unique and for the rest of your career you will be on your own learning journey.

This book supports your journey and development as an early years ECT. We hope it proves an invaluable source of information and inspiration during these formative years of your career.

Good luck.

# Chapter 1   What is it like to be an early years teacher?

## What? (The big idea)

### Finding your feet as an early years teacher

Your career as a teacher begins the moment you step foot into the school where you hope to secure your first teaching role. Following your interview, receiving that all-important telephone call offering you your first teaching position and confirming your acceptance, first verbally and then in writing, sets your early teaching career in motion. Exciting times – congratulations, you are now a teacher and a colleague within a team and a school community! Your initial euphoria may be followed by excited anticipation, which can then dissipate into fear and panic – '*Why did they choose me?*'; '*How will I measure up?*'; '*What if I cannot teach?*' But remember, you have been through a rigorous selection process and have been chosen for a good reason. You have the skills and qualities that complement the school, its values and the existing team. Beauchamp and Thomas (2009, p 175) acknowledge that '*student teachers must undergo a shift in identity as they move through programs of teacher education and assume positions as teachers in today's challenging school contexts'*. You are not alone; your colleagues are there to support you through the highs and lows of your transformational journey as an early career teacher (ECT), a journey perhaps that only those associated with schools may understand. Your colleagues in school will delight with you when a child that you have been working with for weeks has that '*wow*' moment! Equally, they will know first-hand what it means to be 'teacher tired' by the time you make it to half term! All these experiences will shape you as an early years teacher (EYT).

This first chapter supports your journey in the early weeks and then the academic year as you consider your sense of developing identity as an EYT. Interestingly, research conducted by Lightfoot and Frost (2015) found that early years educators (EYEs), regardless of status or role, felt strongly that their professional identity was shaped by making a difference to young children, their families, the settings in which they worked, and their local community. Although you may humbly believe yourself to be 'just' an EYT, you are a vital role model to the children you teach and a key player in the life of the child and their family. While parents or carers certainly would not loan you the keys to their shiny new car or the pin code to their iPhone, they are loaning time with something far more precious – their child. You are in a unique and privileged position to make every moment and every learning experience for that child count. The holistic nature of the Early Years Foundation Stage (EYFS) curriculum and your role as a highly skilled EYT will inevitably mean that you are constantly juggling and wearing many hats. Examples of this can be seen in the practical day-to-day management of the learning environment, where continuous provision offers a range of high-quality, playful learning experiences during which the child can develop skills across the early years (EY) curriculum. A further example can be seen in the expertise, patience and compassion it takes to settle an emotionally upset child in school for the very first time while skilfully and sensitively reassuring a worried parent or carer.

## Keeping those plates spinning

As an EYT you are an action researcher, continually reflecting on your practice to identify areas for development (Abrahamson, 2018). All of these will no doubt influence your emerging identity and your knowledge, skills and attitudes towards being an EYT. There will be times when you need to reflect and respond in the moment as you are working with or observing the children, while other reflections may require a more strategic, action research approach to seek knowledge and understanding of the children and to find new ways in which to work. Being an EYT is a diverse role, which means having a multi-faceted identity. At times it may be time consuming and difficult to switch off from. Mainstone-Cotton (2018) proposes that EY professionals are better equipped to support and enhance children's emotional well-being when they prioritise their own mental health. Therefore, looking after yourself, as well as being supported when necessary by your setting and colleagues, will be key to your future well-being (Howard et al, 2020). Building in time to 'recharge your batteries' – enjoying personal interests and time with family and friends – will become an important balance to establish. Yet, the awe and wonder on a young child's face when they discover something new for the first time or make a giant leap in mastering tricky learning or skills makes the role of the EYT pure magic.

There may be times on your ECT journey and further into your career when it will be important to revisit what inspired you to become an EYT; your 'calling'. This may include your educational philosophy and values; your passion for the EY; as well as what influenced, inspired and motivated you. All these factors will inform your developing identity as an EY ECT. It is important to acknowledge that your identity as an EYT will be constantly changing and evolving through your experiences – these include the professional, personal and cultural (Cox and Teszenyi, 2016). As you gain experience, your confidence will increase and your sense of belonging within the profession will grow (Beauchamp and Thomas, 2009). Nonetheless, expect that there will be moments when changes in your immediate work environment or to EY curriculum and policy may influence your feelings of preparedness. If you find yourself in this place, remember that it is always the children that you need to keep at the heart of your practice. You know the children well and understand their personal learning journey and next steps. You have invested time and care in getting to know the children, their families and the local community. Embracing your own professional learning journey will enable you to develop your EY expertise while considering the importance of establishing yourself within the wider school team. You will value those all-important connections you build with colleagues across the school community and value how these newly forged relationships can support you professionally and personally as an ECT. Establishing your place as a teacher on a wider school team can be challenging for an ECT but a further challenge can be forging your place on the team as an EYT. Often the EY can feel like the forgotten phase and overshadowed by Key Stage (KS) 1 and 2 in a primary school. EY may also be seen as a separate entity to the wider school. There is often a myth in the upper echelons of the school that *'all you do in early years is play!'* Celebrate your identity as an EYT – your passion, pride and sense of purpose. Recognise your value to the children you teach and the wider school community in your setting.

## Why is it interesting? Challenging *'all you do in early years is play!'*

The 'passion and purpose' needed to be an outstanding EY ECT is something that you must be an ambassador for. The way you conduct yourself as a professional will speak volumes about you. The EY workforce, which spans EY practitioners and childcare providers, has long endorsed the need for *'excellence in early years'*

(DfE, 2017). However, as Osgood et al (2017) propose, the status of EYTs is often undervalued. This may be compounded by the fact that training and qualification pathways into EY careers are varied; differing in status, pay and future career prospects. In the midst and aftermath of the Covid-19 pandemic and its impact on our early learners, it could be argued that we need the most dynamic, creative and effective teachers in EY settings. As Tymms et al (2018) concur, the strongest teachers should be placed in EY classrooms, where their impact upon young learners will lay the robust foundations needed for future success and life opportunities.

Whether it is said in jest or is a misconception of a colleague or parent/carer, EYTs do much more than 'play'. It can be a real challenge to alter this, sometimes fixed, perception of your role. Remember first and foremost you are an EY expert, an advocate of EY practice and pedagogy. If you ever doubt this, consider carefully how child development can be related to aspects of your classroom practice, whether it is the way you support children through building purposeful and secure attachments or scaffold and support systematic synthetic phonics and early number. When you reflect upon this, you will realise that every aspect of your practice is underpinned with knowledge of how children learn and develop. Play and playful experiences are not incidental; they are facilitated by you as the EYT to support the child's learning and development across the holistic EYFS curriculum.

Play has long been a subject of interest within EY pedagogy and research. There has been a real desire to understand the philosophy of play; to define the dimensions of play and its importance in relation to a child's learning and development. Given the breadth of this subject, this desire to understand play will continue to evolve. Your growing knowledge of 'play' and 'play pedagogy' will support you to build expertise and enhance your excellent practice. A great deal of research and theory discusses how play can support children to develop cognitively, personally, socially, emotionally, linguistically, physically, as well as creatively. All of these are aspects seen in the Early Learning Goals (ELG) within the EYFS (DfE, 2021). As Grindheim and Odegaard (2013) concede, there is an intrinsic link between play and learning in the EY.

Seminal works such as Piaget's (1936) theory of play continue to be used in education to understand the cognitive development of children through four developmental play stages:

1.  sensorimotor stage (birth to 2 years);

2.  preoperational stage (ages 2 to 7);

3.  concrete operational stage (ages 7 to 11);

4.  formal operational stage (ages 12 and up).

Piaget's (1936) work however was not without criticism by his contemporaries. Vygotsky (1978) and Bruner (1960) – both social constructivists – believed that learning and knowledge was constructed through social interactions. They were not convinced that these stages of play and development should be seen as fixed, preferring to regard them as a continuous process of development. The importance of collaboration, social interaction and learning from a more knowledgeable other (MKO) was crucial to cognitive development, according to Vygotsky (1978). Bruner (1960) however favoured the notion that children learn through discovery based on experiences and therefore anything can be learnt by a child at any stage through the concept of the spiral curriculum. It is important to remember that play and learning theories are still being expanded upon and developed as educationists and psychologists seek to understand and make sense of the importance of play within a child's development.

Play in all its forms can be fun and rewarding for children, whether a solitary, parallel or collaborative activity. Play can be a powerful tool which helps children to make sense of the adult world and its cultural expectations, values, rules and norms. 'Play therapy' is even used as a therapeutic device which enables children to work through lived traumatic experiences. Equally, play is not limited by the resources children have access to – imagination is limitless. Children growing up in deprivation or challenging circumstances find ways of innovating, creating games and imaginative play scenarios with others and with the objects they may find and the environment around them. Play is a means of problem solving and finding solutions. In much the same way, adults seek to solve problems through 'playing', tinkering and experimenting, demonstrating resilience to overcome barriers, innovating and applying creative processes. 'Play' also fuels adult creativity and imagination, such as in the games design industry. Whether conceptualising, designing and creating, playing games for educational purposes or playing games purely for entertainment and enjoyment, 'play' is a central theme with 'learning' intrinsically linked to the notion of play.

In your EYT role, it is imperative to focus on the learning child and relate your knowledge of child development to your practice. The learning environment is integral to the Reggio Emilia Approach, often described as 'the third teacher', harnessing children's natural curiosities, interest in the world around them and their developmental stage through its design, resources and exploratory opportunities. Hewitt (2001, p 96) expresses that within the approach, 'the child is beheld as beautiful, powerful, competent, creative, curious, and full of potential and ambitious desires' and that the child possesses the capacity to develop their own learning potential. Have confidence in your convictions – play is an integral part of learning and development. As famously said by Maria Montessori (1986), 'play is the work of the child'. Stay true to your strong identity as an EYT and professional, sharing your EY knowledge and expertise of how young children develop and learn. This will empower you to disseminate good practice, build connections with professionals and feel established and confident within the wider school team. It will also be important to examine how your role as an ECT in EY provides the 'foundation' for children's later success as they move through their school life. If these foundations are not secure, then failure will inevitably follow. It is not called the 'foundation' stage without good reason. Nothing with any stability or durability can be built without strong and robust foundations.

## Reflective task ◀◀◀

- How do you define play?

- Why do you believe play is important to children?

- How will you incorporate play into your EY learning environment?

- How will you justify the play experiences within your classroom?

- What would you say to a parent, carer or colleague who suggests that 'all you do in EY is play'?

# So what?

## What difference does it make?

## Reflective task ◀◀◀

### Teacher identity handprint

Exploring your identity as an EYT is vitally important. It is easy to forget what originally inspired and motivated you to choose an EY teaching career. Think about your journey so far.

- Pick five words that best describe how you see yourself as an EYT. With each word, consider why you chose it and how it fits against your ideal of an EYT. An example is provided in Table 1.1, together with further space for you to add your own five words.

**Table 1.1 Teacher identity key words**

| Word to describe yourself as an EYT | Why is this word important to you? | How does it fit with your ideal of an EYT? |
|---|---|---|
| Patient | Patience is a key quality of an effective teacher. | • EY children may need time to secure new learning.<br><br>• Concepts may need to be revisited or practised several times before they become secure.<br><br>• Developmentally, children may be at various stages within their learning and development. |
| 1. | | |
| 2. | | |
| 3. | | |
| 4. | | |
| 5. | | |

- Now write these five words on the fingertips on the handprint provided below. You may wish to make an enlarged copy of the blank handprint image in Figure 1.1.

**Figure 1.1 Blank teacher identity handprint**

- Next, move to the palm of the handprint and consider how your journey into teaching has shaped you as an EY ECT so far. Reflect upon what led you to become an EYT, your educational values and philosophy. Write about your journey on the palm of the handprint using the prompts below to expand upon your thoughts and feelings.

- Jot down what you believe are the qualities of a good teacher. Which of these do you possess?

- What is special to you about being an EYT and which key people or events have influenced your choice to become an EYT?

- How will you shape children's values and what future impact can you, as an EYT, have on the children you teach?

- What kind of role model do you hope to be?

- How will your beliefs and values shape the learning environment and the opportunities that you provide to the children?

- How can you as an EYT share and disseminate EY pedagogy and practice with other colleagues?

- How can you as an EYT share and disseminate EY pedagogy and practice and have an impact on the wider team, parents/carers and community?

- How can an EYT contribute to a 'community of practice' in EY and beyond?

Figure 1.2 is an example of a completed 'teacher identity handprint' by Javid; it demonstrates how you can approach this reflective task.

**Top tip:** If ever you feel lost on your ECT journey (or beyond), return to your 'teacher identity handprint'. It is a pertinent reminder of your 'passion and purpose' as an EYT and professional.

The handprint contains the following words on the fingers and thumb:

Kind

Inclusive

Enthusiastic

Resilient

Patient

And the following text on the palm:

Kindness first.
I hope to be a compassionate and empathetic EY teacher. I want to make a difference to children's futures, as my Year 1 teacher did. I was a timid child who did not settle well until my Year 1 teacher changed everything. Kind, caring and joyful – I skipped to school every day. Lessons were exciting. Learning left me wide eyed, wanting to find out more. Inspirational teachers in my education made an imprint and shaped the kind of teacher I hope to be. Some were energetic and fun, while others were calm and thought-provoking. All shared a passion to educate, inspire and instil a hunger for learning. Patience, commitment and resilience are qualities and skills I aspire to as an EY teacher. I wish to motivate children to overcome barriers to learning, as my teachers did. I will model values of inclusivity and mutual respect to the children in my care. Enquiry and problem solving will be encouraged with opportunities for children to explore, play, learn and reach their potential. A nurturing and safe learning environment, where every child's voice is valued and positive relationships flourish. I hope to be a valued part of a team, supporting every child and contributing to the wider school ethos and values.

**Figure 1.2 Completed teacher identity handprint**

# Now what? ◀◀◀

## Practical ways to implement this in the classroom

## Practical task for tomorrow ◀◀◀

Consider the importance of the wider team of staff in your setting and the impact these individuals have on you and your practice. Many of your colleagues will be key to your role, for example: supporting transition (Year 1 teacher), the designated safeguarding lead (DSL), Special Educational Needs and Disabilities Co-ordinator (SENDCo), maths and English subject leads.

- Are you confident in being able to approach them for support if needed?

- If not, consider why not?

- Complete your own version of Table 1.2 below which enables you to gather valuable information about key colleagues. An example is provided.

Table 1.2  Key colleagues' roles

| Title of key colleague | Why is their role important within the school? | When might you need to seek their support? | How will you approach them and what will you need to provide? |
|---|---|---|---|
| **English co-ordinator** | *Ensures progression in English skills throughout the school.*<br><br>*Leads the tracking of pupil progress, analysing data and overseeing interventions for key children.*<br><br>*Supports the staff team with planning, delivery and assessment in English and phonics.*<br><br>*Resources, leads and organises continuing professional development (CPD).* | *Support with phonics – planning and training for the chosen phonics scheme. Throughout the year, ensuring children are progressing at key points in phonics, reading and writing.*<br><br>*End-of-year EYFS moderation to make judgements as to whether a child is 'emerging' or 'expected'.*<br><br>*Highlight and raise awareness of where any pupil may have a challenge or potential barrier to learning as early as possible.* | *Make contact early on in my role and work alongside this colleague at key points in the year. Provide planning, examples of children's work, observations and notes from focused activities, children's learning journeys, tracking data.* |

| Title of key colleague | Why is their role important within the school? | When might you need to seek their support? | How will you approach them and what will you need to provide? |
|---|---|---|---|
| EY phase lead/ co-ordinator | | | |
| Year 1/2 teacher | | | |
| Pre-school manager | | | |
| SENDCo | | | |
| DSL | | | |
| ECT mentor | | | |
| Key Stage 1 phase lead/ co-ordinator | | | |
| Subject-specific lead/co-ordinator – English | | | |
| Subject-specific lead/co-ordinator – maths | | | |
| Senior leadership team (SLT) | | | |
| Other | | | |

# Practical task for next week ◀◀◀

Contact colleagues in other schools and EY settings in the local area. Becoming part of a wider network of EY practitioners can provide invaluable opportunities to support one another, share ideas, experiences and practices that will shape you as an EYT. This can be particularly important if you are an EYT in a single-form entry school. Creating this network can also help to understand yourself (your own identity and your place within your setting and the wider professional community), the local community, the children and families and EY provision available. For example, a child may be transitioning into your class from a pre-school setting or childcare provider that is not part of your school's usual catchment; therefore, an existing relationship with this child's setting would support the child and family when moving on to your school. Forming relationships with others could be a useful connection when you are trying to improve a certain aspect of your practice, eg you are hoping to develop your outdoor classroom and would like to visit a setting with outstanding provision. Keep a record of colleagues from other EY settings by completing Table 1.3. An example has been provided for you.

**Table 1.3  Key information about other EY settings**

| Name and type of setting | EY professional's role and name<br><br>(eg EYT, phase lead, EY practitioner) | How can this link be supportive to me?<br><br>(strengths or attributes of the setting, eg Forest School area, school feeder setting) | What can I do to develop the links? |
|---|---|---|---|
| Froglets Pre-school<br><br>Pre-school – children aged 2–4 years<br><br>Term-time provision 8am–3.30pm | EY pre-school manager<br><br>EY practitioners | Link setting for children entering Reception | Organise a regular time in the Spring/ Summer term for either myself or TA to go and read a story to the children and meet the families in preparation for school starters in September. |
| | | | |
| | | | |
| | | | |
| | | | |
| | | | |
| | | | |

Reflect upon how your identity as an EYT has changed because of all you have experienced. Think about when and how you can share your amazing practice and the children's successes with the wider team over the next academic year. Use the headings in Table 1.4 to plan how you will share three elements of your practice and when and who you will disseminate your practice to, whether in staff meetings or inviting colleagues, parents and carers to your EY classroom to get involved with exciting teaching and learning. Do not be afraid to shine and share your good EY practice!

**Table 1.4 Elements of practice**

| Element of practice | Opportunity to share practice *Example:* Developing children's gross and fine motor skills in preparation for handwriting acquisition. | Opportunity to share practice |
|---|---|---|
| **Intent:** | | |
| Why is this important to share? | Colleagues will better understand the Early Learning Goals within the prime area of Physical Development (DfE, 2021) and the important relationship between gross motor control of large movements and how this supports children to develop fine motor control and later skill in handwriting. | 1.<br><br>2. |
| | This may still be an area of development for some children as they move through school, which may have an impact on their letter formation, handwriting fluency and legibility. | 3. |
| **Implementation:** | | |
| How can I share this practice? | Invite colleagues to the EY learning environment – showcase activities in the enabling environment that support gross motor development, eg balance bikes, mini yoga, wobble boards, and fine motor control activities, eg threading, play-doh, mixed media mark-making opportunities. | 1.<br><br>2. |
| | Show examples of handwriting development, photographs of children writing – pencil grip, pressure on paper etc. | 3. |

| Element of practice | Opportunity to share practice<br>*Example:*<br>*Developing children's gross and fine motor skills in preparation for handwriting acquisition.* | Opportunity to share practice |
|---|---|---|
| When will I share this practice? | *During a staff meeting or TED.* | 1.<br><br>2.<br><br>3. |
| Who will I share this practice with? | *Teachers and teaching assistants in Key Stage 1 and 2.* | 1.<br><br>2.<br><br>3. |
| **Impact:** | | |
| What will the impact be on others? | *Knowledge and understanding of some of the barriers to learning that some children may continue to experience when writing.*<br><br>*Practical suggestions to support children's handwriting development.* | 1.<br><br>2.<br><br>3. |
| What will the impact be on the children? | *Children moving through school, who still find fine motor control challenging can be supported with their next step in this area. This may have a far-reaching impact as handwriting is a key skill.* | 1.<br><br>2.<br><br>3. |
| What will the impact be on me? | *Confidence to contribute and disseminate EY expertise within the team.*<br><br>*Greater understanding from colleagues about the role of the EYT and the importance of developing this skill for children.* | 1.<br><br>2.<br><br>3. |

# What next? ◀ ◀ ◀

This chapter has outlined what it is like to be an EYT. It has shown the many facets to your developing identity as an EYT. Engaging with further reading will consolidate this and fuel your 'passion and purpose' as an advocate of EY education, pedagogy and practice.

## Further reading

Bottrill, G (2018) *Can I Go and Play Now? Rethinking the Early Years*. 1st ed. London: Sage.

Cox, A and Sykes, G (2016) *The Multiple Identities of a Reception Teacher*. London: Sage.

Palaiologoa, I (2016) *The Early Years Foundation Stage: Theory and Practice*. 3rd ed. Los Angeles: Sage.

## References

Abrahamson, L (2018) *The Early Years Teacher's Handbook.* London: Sage.

Beauchamp, C and Thomas, L (2009) Understanding Teacher Identity: An Overview of Issues in the Literature and Implications for Teacher Education. *Cambridge Journal of Education*, 39(2): 175–89.

Bruner, J S (1960) *The Process of Education*. Cambridge, MA: Harvard University Press.

Cox, A and Teszenyi, E (2016) Time Travel, Kaleidoscopes and a Hat Shop. In Cox, A and Sykes, G (eds) *The Multiple Identities of a Reception Teacher*. Los Angeles: Learning Matters.

Department of Education (DfE) (2017) *Early Years Workforce Strategy*. London: Crown.

Department for Education (DfE) (2021) *Statutory Framework for the Early Years Foundation Stage*. London: Department for Education.

Grindheim, L and Odegaard, E (2013) What Is the State of Play? *International Journal of Play*, 2(1): 4–6.

Hewitt, V (2001) Examining the Reggio Emilia Approach to Early Childhood Education. *Early Childhood Education Journal*, 29(2): 95–100.

Howard, C, Burton, M and Levermore, D (2020) *Children's Mental Health and Emotional Well-being in Primary Schools: A Whole School Approach*. 2nd ed. London: Learning Matters/Sage.

Lightfoot, S and Frost, D (2015) The Professional Identity of Early Years Educators in England: Implications for a Transformative Approach to Continuing Professional Development. *Professional Development in Education*, 41(2): 401–18.

Mainstone-Cotton, S (2018) *Promoting Emotional Wellbeing in Early Years Staff.* London: Jessica Kingsley Publishers.

Montessori, M (1986) *The Discovery of the Child*. New York: Ballantine Books.

Osgood, J, Elwick, A, Robertson, L, Sakr, M and Wilson, D (2017) *Early Years Teacher and Early Years Educator: A Scoping Study of the Impact, Experiences and Associated Issues of Recent Early Years Qualifications and Training in England.* [online] Available at: www.mdx.ac.uk/__data/assets/pdf_file/0019/363313/Early-Years-Teacher-and-Early-Years-Educator.pdf (accessed 13 August 2022).

Piaget, J (1936) *Origins of Intelligence in the Child.* London: Routledge & Kegan Paul.

Tymms, P, Merrell, C and Bailey, K (2018) The Long-Term Impact of Effective Teaching. *School Effectiveness and School Improvement*, 29(2): 242–61.

Vygotsky, L (1978) *Mind in Society: The Development of Higher Psychological Processes.* Cambridge, MA: Harvard University Press.

# Chapter 2   How to promote outstanding provision and purposeful assessment

# What? (The big idea)

## Building early years expertise

This chapter considers the statutory and non-statutory Early Years Foundation Stage (EYFS) documents that support you to plan for progression and facilitate a holistic early years (EY) curriculum which enables young children to flourish. It reflects upon the efficacy of the Reception Baseline Assessment (RBA) when teamed with your own teacher observations and assessments to build a profile of each child's learning and progress. This growing knowledge supports you as an early years teacher (EYT) to facilitate and plan for vital next steps in securing pupil success. The chapter also promotes a personal consideration of the fundamental importance of developing as an EY expert as you move through your early career teacher (ECT) period, including the ways in which you can develop your EY subject knowledge and transform your practice through understanding a child's development across the EYFS prime and specific areas of learning. Further consideration is given to the range of ongoing assessment strategies that form part of your EYFS practice (observation, anecdotal and more formalised assessment procedures) and enable you to advance pupil progress through planning for outstanding provision within the holistic EY curriculum.

## The big early years puzzle picture

The 'holistic' EY curriculum is a term that is frequently used, but what does this mean in practice? Simply put, the term 'holistic' emphasises the importance of an interconnected EY curriculum that supports a child's rounded development, not only cognitively but also through their personal, social, spiritual, physical and emotional growth. McDowall-Clark (2020) recognises that when adopting child-centred approaches the focus shifts from curriculum content to the child. Education is shaped, starting with the child as an individual by responding to their needs and interests, with an emphasis on learning through play, as opposed to being teacher directed or subject-content driven. Policy makers in the EY sector steering pedagogy and practice have long recognised the importance of establishing a play-based foundation stage and its crucial link to the learning and development of three to five year-olds (Miller and Hevey, 2012). This is reflected within the EYFS, giving equal importance to all areas of learning and development and recognising how these areas are interconnected. The statutory framework for the EYFS (DfE, 2021a) focuses on seven areas of learning and development that shape EY education.

There are three prime areas of learning:

1. communication and language;

2. physical development;

3. personal, social and emotional development.

There are four specific areas of learning:

1. literacy;

2. mathematics;

3. understanding the world;

4. expressive arts and design.

The prime areas are described as important foundations for children which support the specific areas of learning (DfE, 2021a). An example of this can be seen in the prime area of learning: physical development, through two Early Learning Goals (ELGs): gross motor skills and fine motor skills. Both ELGs are interconnected and paramount to a child's physical development which, in turn supports the ELG: writing, in the literacy specific area of learning. Within these prime and specific areas of learning there are a total of 17 ELGs which children work towards throughout the Foundation Stage period and culminate at the end of a child's Reception year. As an EYT you are required to make 'holistic' best-fit judgements of a child's attainment within these 17 ELGs (DfE, 2021a). The EYFS statutory framework (DfE, 2021a) advocates the child-centred pedagogical approach, highlighted earlier in this chapter, in which the interactions between the EY practitioner and the child sustain and extend child-initiated learning and activities (Fitzgerald and Kay, 2016). However, this can be a balancing act for you as an EYT, trying to achieve harmony between child-initiated and teacher-led opportunities within your classroom practice to ensure that children successfully progress in all areas of learning. Your understanding of the EY curriculum, alongside your ever-evolving knowledge of the children, will support you to plan and facilitate meaningful learning opportunities where children's skills can be developed.

# Reflective task ◀◀◀

Are you confident in your understanding of the EYFS curriculum, the prime and specific areas and the ELGs? Your practice will be guided through developing your depth of understanding. As you explore the statutory framework for the EYFS (DfE, 2021a), jot down your responses to the following questions:

- How confident are you about understanding progression in this area?

- What other ELGs does this connect to in a child's development?

- Where can this practice be seen in your setting?

- How can you develop this ELG to support the children's progress?

Your understanding of the EYFS curriculum teamed with your knowledge of the children in your class will support you to promote outstanding provision. Consider the following questions:

- How well do you know the children in your care?

- What do you know about their interests and enthusiasms?

- What are their individual and collective areas of strength and development?

- How can their interests, enthusiasms, strengths and areas of development be built into your planning and provision in the learning environment?

## Top tips ◀◀◀

- As you get to know the children's interests and enthusiasms, make these the heart of your planning.

- Use planning 'in the moment' to extend a child's learning and thinking as they are exploring continuous provision activities. An example of this would involve conversing with or observing a child who is trying to solve a problem and offering resources which will support them to independently further their understanding and reach a solution. Planning in the moment is explored further in Chapter 4: 'How to create a successful enabling learning environment'.

- Build the focus of your planning for the day, week, term or across the academic year around your growing knowledge of the children's topics and areas of interest.

- Planning with the children can be an effective way to harness their voice, support them to make connections and move their learning forward across all areas of the learning. For example, share the next topic with the children in advance, so that you can incorporate their ideas for the role play area, writing corner, construction area and outdoor learning environment planning and preparation.

## Pieces of the puzzle

Being able to plan and facilitate outstanding provision in the EY takes great skill, expertise and understanding of the pupils' learning and development. In Reception this begins formally with the new RBA, which was introduced to all Reception pupils starting school in September 2021 and focuses on early mathematics, literacy, communication and language. You will need to complete the RBA in the first six weeks of a child's Reception journey. This will provide you with a starting point for Reception cohorts which can later be compared to Key Stage 2 outcomes. Although the RBA is not used to judge EY provision, it can support early baseline information for you as an EYT (DfE, 2021a). However, gaining a baseline of each pupil is nothing new to EY practitioners working with children across the Foundation Stage. It has long been deemed good practice to gather evidence from a range of sources, such as anecdotal evidence from practitioners in previous settings, parents and carers and observation strategies. The *Development*

*Matters* non-statutory guidance for the EYFS (DfE, 2021b) will support you as well as other practitioners across the EY sector (EY practitioners, childminders, nursery settings and Reception classes) to design an effective curriculum that builds on the strengths and next steps of the children in your care. This document underpins the statutory framework for the EYFS (DfE, 2021a), presenting children's developmental pathways in broad ages and stages. *Development Matters* can support you as an EYT to make informed decisions about a child's next steps in learning and how you can promote children's thinking skills (Abrahamson, 2018). However, it should be acknowledged that this guidance stipulates that young children's learning is not *'neat and orderly'* and that ensuring *'accurate and proportionate assessment is vital'* (DfE, 2021b, p 4). This is something that you may already be acutely aware of from working with children in your EY class. You may be able to think of tangible examples which illustrate how children's learning and progress is not straightforward or linear.

Transition and induction periods can also assist you in getting to know the child in all areas of the EYFS – their interests, strengths and areas for development. Your conversations with previous EY settings and childcare providers to support transition will inevitably focus on the Characteristics of Effective Teaching and Learning (CoETL) (DfE, 2021a, p 16):

> *Three characteristics of effective teaching and learning are:*
>
> » *playing and exploring – children investigate and experience things, and 'have a go'*
>
> » *active learning – children concentrate and keep on trying if they encounter difficulties, and enjoy achievements*
>
> » *creating and thinking critically – children have and develop their own ideas, make links between ideas, and develop strategies for doing things.*

To learn well, children need to explore learning through meaningful contexts and opportunities that ignite curiosity and enthusiasm. The CoETL (DfE, 2021a) gives you the tools to better understand a child's learning behaviours, arming you with a wealth of knowledge surrounding how an individual child enjoys exploring and engaging with their learning environment. Intrinsically linked to the CoETL are the four overarching principles of the EYFS outlined in the statutory framework for EYFS (DfE, 2021a):

1. unique child;

2. positive relationships;

3. enabling environments with teaching and support from adults;

4. learning and development.

Children learn in response to the *'positive relationships'* they build, and the learning opportunities supported by adults in *'the enabling environment'* that allow them to flourish as a *'unique child'*. The fourth principle recognises the fundamental importance of *'learning and development'*, which happens at different rates for the individual.

The many pieces of the puzzle support you as an EY ECT to skilfully plan, design and facilitate opportunities for children to develop and refine skills, knowledge and understanding, aiding their progress and personal learning journey. Most importantly, do not forget the child themselves in this process; their voice can provide you with a wealth of information which supports you to enhance skills and knowledge through facilitating learning and play experiences (Williams, 2021).

## Reflective task ◀◀◀

- Now that you have a deeper understanding of the EYFS curriculum, look further at the *Development Matters* non-statutory guidance (DfE, 2021b). How can this further support your EY expertise and practice?

- Why are the CoETL important in EY?

- How will you build the CoETL into your daily practice?

- Give examples of how each of the EYFS four overarching principles are reflected through practice in your EY setting.

## Assessment: an integral puzzle component

Planning, teaching and assessing the many facets of the EYFS curriculum can be a challenge to manage as an ECT. As you move forward and grow your expertise in the EYFS holistic curriculum, you will hone your skills in planning to support the whole child. Your developing knowledge of the EYFS and the developing child work in tandem to support you to plan effectively to meet the next steps in learning and progression towards the ELGs by the end of the Reception year. Continual formative assessment and planning are two key puzzle pieces that are intrinsically linked.

Assessment in EY is so much more than testing children's knowledge and understanding. You will work closely with teaching assistants (TAs) in your setting to review children's progress and their next steps as part of the continual assessment and planning cycle. This ongoing process informs what you will teach, the opportunities you will facilitate through continuous provision, and how you will support children, daily and often 'in the moment', to acquire and develop skills and extend knowledge (Dubiel, 2014). Observation is a key EY assessment strategy which should be used to respond to young children and support the next stage in their development (Tickell, 2011). As an EYT it is your responsibility to carefully observe and learn from what you see in order to enrich and extend children's learning (Smidt, 2015). What you know about the children should influence your planning. Bottrill (2020, pp 64–5) describes this as *'next steps planning'* in which children should be offered some freedom and the opportunity to make connections in their learning and refine skills, while exploring next steps in a way that ignites intrigue and curiosity. Your role as an EYT is collaborative and as you discover more about the children, planning evolves in response to all that you know and have yet to discover about them.

## Reflective task ◀◀◀

Consider the use of observation as an assessment strategy in your EY practice.

- How is observation used in your practice?

- When is observation a useful assessment tool?

- Who is involved in observing children?

- How does observation feed into planning?

## Top tips ◀◀◀

- Build time into your week where you can be a 'fly on the wall' and observe children's child-initiated play in the learning environment.

- Capture observations of play in photographs, through annotations, and in video or audio recordings. These can be evidenced in learning journeys, capturing a child's progress in all EYFS areas of learning.

- Work collaboratively with TAs so that they too are empowered to observe and record these observations of children's learning and progress.

Additionally, sustained shared thinking (SST) can be an effective tool in your EY assessment which can help you to plan effectively with the learner at the heart of your practice. The principle of SST is defined as:

*an episode in which two or more individuals 'work together' in an intellectual way to solve a problem, clarify a concept, evaluate activities, extend a narrative etc. Both parties must contribute to the thinking and it must develop and extend.*

(Sylva et al, 2004, p 36)

It may involve conversation and collaboration between adult and child or peer-on-peer interaction. Essentially, this two-way dialogue supports you as the teacher to learn from the child and use this knowledge to collaboratively extend children's thinking and depth of understanding. As an EYT, SST requires you to engage in 'active listening' as well as modelling 'thinking' processes out loud. Establishing an SST ethos requires time and commitment from children and adults alike, where exchanges in conversation and discussion are valued. Imperatively, research demonstrates that outcomes are improved across children's holistic development when SST principles are applied to EY practice (Brodie, 2014).

The following case study depicts SST in action between Niamh and two children in her class, Ben (age four) and Tia (age five):

## Case study ◀◀◀

Niamh and her children are looking at fossils in the investigation area of the classroom.

Tia (child):       *What kind of stone is that?*

Niamh (teacher): *It's called a fossil.*

Tia (child):       *It looks like bones.*

Niamh (teacher): *Some people think it might be a dinosaur. What do you think?*

Tia (child):       *It's a dinosaur.*

Niamh (teacher): *How do you know?*

Tia (child):       *It just looks like it.*

Niamh (teacher): *What do you think this part is here?* [pointing to the head]

Ben (child):       *It's the head.*

Niamh (teacher): *What makes you say that? What can you see?*

Ben (child):       *It's got holes for the eyes.*

Tia (child): *That looks like a nose [pointing to a skull shape]. It looks old.*

Niamh (teacher): *How can you tell it's old?*

Ben (child): *It's very dirty.*

Niamh (teacher): *You are right; it does look very dirty. Where do you think it was found?*

Ben (child): *In the mud?*

Tia (child): *I think it was found inside rocks.*

## Reflective task ◀◀◀

- How did Niamh's questions support the children to make sense of the world?

- How did Niamh extend the children's thinking?

- What other questions could Niamh ask to engage the children further?

- What learning opportunities might Niamh offer to extend learning further?

- How will Niamh use this understanding of the children in her assessment of their learning and development?

Reflecting on the case study provided and your own experiences in your classroom, consider the usefulness of SST in your practice.

- What opportunities are there in your everyday practice to implement SST?

- Who will be involved in SST?

- How will you encourage an SST ethos in your classroom?

- How can SST be used to assess understanding and inform your planning?

## Top tips ◀◀◀

- Posing questions which stimulate children to think philosophically can be a great starting point for SST, eg *What is it like to be a hamster?*; *If you could invent a machine what would it do?*; *What superpower is the most important and why?*

- Taking a step away and listening in to children's conversations with peers can provide a wealth of knowledge that you can then extend through planning opportunities that challenge and stretch children's thinking.

- SST does not always need to be planned for; it is often those incidental exchanges when a child arrives at school, during morning snack or at story time.

## Completing the puzzle

Information for the assessment of young children is gathered in a variety of ways:

» careful observation of the children as they interact with others and their learning environment;

» through rich dialogue with the children themselves;

» gleaning information and knowledge from a range of people who know the children well;

» examples of children's work and recorded formative progress assessments in specific areas of learning such as phonics or number.

In EY practice, learning journeys are an effective tool to document a child's progress through the EYFS. These can be physical portfolios with photographs, examples of work, annotations and assessments or virtual electronic learning journeys, eg Tapestry, Evidence Me by 2simple, designed to link the ELGs and CoETL. Whatever method you choose, learning journeys should be shared regularly with parents and carers to inform them of their child's engagement with the EYFS curriculum and to provide a basis for your conversations about next steps. This evidence also supports you as an EYT to form secure judgements about whether a child is 'emerging' (not yet meeting expectations) or 'expected' (meeting expectations) within each of the 17 ELGs at the end of the Reception year. A good level of development (GLD) is achieved if children are assessed at 'expected' levels in the prime areas of development and the specific areas of maths and literacy (DfE, 2022). The information you gather forms the summative Early Years Foundation Stage Profile (EYFSP), which is shared with parents/carers and discussed with Year 1 teachers to support successful transition. Within your class, children who are 'emerging' will continue to be supported as they transition into Year 1. Your EYFSP data for all children completing their Reception year, including those with SEND (Special Educational Needs and Disabilities) and EAL (English as an additional language), is shared with the local authority upon request in late June of each academic year. The local authority is then responsible for returning this data to the DfE (DfE, 2021a). The ongoing formative assessments that you have accumulated over the year, alongside your extensive knowledge of the individual, will support you to make sound judgements for each child in each ELG. As an EYT in a Reception class, you will need to understand recording and reporting procedures for the EYFSP and the *Reception Baseline Assessment and Reporting Arrangements* (DfE, 2021c). Further guidance in the EYFSP handbook (DfE, 2022) has been produced to help you to make accurate judgements about each child's level of development at the end of the EYFS. On completion of a child's Reception year, you will need to summarise attainment in relation to the 17 ELG descriptors, including a short narrative describing the child's CoETL. This information will frame conversations with Year 1 teachers, SENDCos and parents/carers to support the child's transition into Key Stage 1. Remember, you are not alone in making these professional judgements about what each child knows, can do and understands. It is good practice to moderate with colleagues in school and other EYTs across different schools. This supportive moderation process will ensure that your judgements are in line with other settings. Inevitably, by the end of the academic year you will be very much the EY expert and the absolute expert of the children in your care and the journey that they have been on!

# So what? ◀◀◀

## What difference does it make?

## Reflective task ◀◀◀

Assessment is not something that only applies to the children you teach. There are times when you may need to assess your own knowledge, understanding and practice. Make your continuing professional development a personal priority as an EY ECT and as you progress through your career. As a reflective EYT, you will be continually reviewing your practice and seeking opportunities to enhance your knowledge, understanding and expertise in your field. Reviews with your mentor will support you to carve out a pathway of progress. The following reflective task will help you prepare for review conversations.

- Consider the questions in the blank professional development mind map shown in Figure 2.1. Use these as prompts for your reflections upon an area of subject knowledge, EYFS principles or pedagogical practice.

- Now complete your own professional development mind map. An example is given in Figure 2.2.

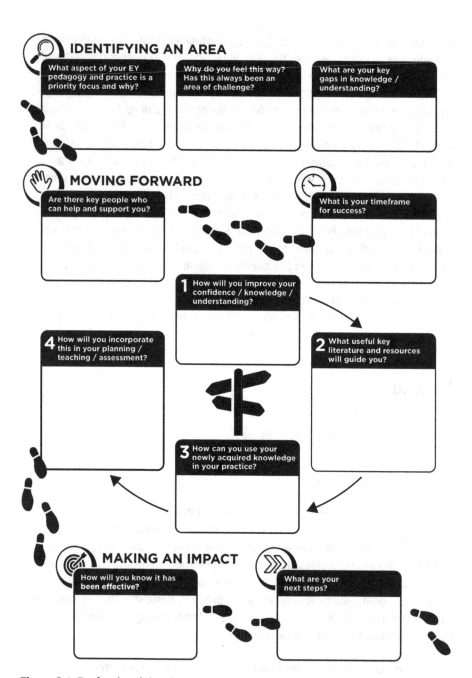

**IDENTIFYING AN AREA**

What aspect of your EY pedagogy and practice is a priority focus and why?

Why do you feel this way? Has this always been an area of challenge?

What are your key gaps in knowledge / understanding?

**MOVING FORWARD**

Are there key people who can help and support you?

What is your timeframe for success?

1 How will you improve your confidence / knowledge / understanding?

2 What useful key literature and resources will guide you?

4 How will you incorporate this in your planning / teaching / assessment?

3 How can you use your newly acquired knowledge in your practice?

**MAKING AN IMPACT**

How will you know it has been effective?

What are your next steps?

Figure 2.1  Professional development mind map template

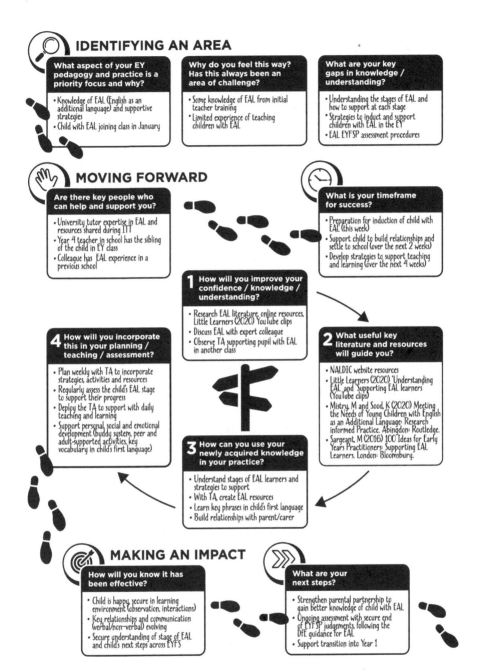

## IDENTIFYING AN AREA

**What aspect of your EY pedagogy and practice is a priority focus and why?**

- Knowledge of EAL (English as an additional language) and supportive strategies
- Child with EAL joining class in January

**Why do you feel this way? Has this always been an area of challenge?**

- Some knowledge of EAL from initial teacher training
- Limited experience of teaching children with EAL

**What are your key gaps in knowledge / understanding?**

- Understanding the stages of EAL and how to support at each stage
- Strategies to induct and support children with EAL in the EY
- EAL EYFSP assessment procedures

## MOVING FORWARD

**Are there key people who can help and support you?**

- University tutor expertise in EAL and resources shared during ITT
- Year 4 teacher in school has the sibling of the child in EY class
- Colleague has EAL experience in a previous school

**What is your timeframe for success?**

- Preparation for induction of child with EAL (this week)
- Support child to build relationships and settle to school (over the next 2 weeks)
- Develop strategies to support teaching and learning (over the next 4 weeks)

**1 How will you improve your confidence / knowledge / understanding?**

- Research EAL literature, online resources, Little Learners (2020) YouTube clips
- Discuss EAL with expert colleague
- Observe TA supporting pupil with EAL in another class

**2 What useful key literature and resources will guide you?**

- NALDIC website resources
- Little Learners (2020) 'Understanding EAL' and 'Supporting EAL learners' (YouTube clips)
- Mistry, M and Sood, K (2020) Meeting the Needs of Young Children with English as an Additional Language: Research informed Practice. Abingdon: Routledge.
- Sargeant, M (2016) 100 Ideas for Early Years Practitioners: Supporting EAL Learners. London: Bloomsbury.

**4 How will you incorporate this in your planning / teaching / assessment?**

- Plan weekly with TA to incorporate strategies, activities and resources
- Regularly assess the child's EAL stage to support their progress
- Deploy the TA to support with daily teaching and learning
- Support personal, social and emotional development (buddy system, peer and adult-supported activities, key vocabulary in child's first language)

**3 How can you use your newly acquired knowledge in your practice?**

- Understand stages of EAL learners and strategies to support
- With TA, create EAL resources
- Learn key phrases in child's first language
- Build relationships with parent/carer

## MAKING AN IMPACT

**How will you know it has been effective?**

- Child is happy, secure in learning environment (observation, interactions)
- Key relationships and communication (verbal/non-verbal) evolving
- Secure understanding of stage of EAL and child's next steps across EYFS

**What are your next steps?**

- Strengthen parental partnership to gain better knowledge of child with EAL
- Ongoing assessment with secure end of EYFSP judgements, following the DfE guidance for EAL
- Support transition into Year 1

**Figure 2.2 Example of a completed professional development mind map**

- Reflecting upon both yours and the example professional development mind map, is there anything further you can add to support your development and knowledge in your chosen area of pedagogy and practice? What other avenues could you explore?

## Top tips ◀◀◀

Here are some suggestions of resources you could explore:

- links to supportive materials/resources/literature;
- CPD;
- blogs;
- EY forums;
- literature;
- colleagues/co-ordinator in school;
- partnership with other settings;
- experts in university;
- other EY colleagues;
- visits to settings.

The professional development mind map is a useful tool to visit half-termly. Choosing new priority areas for your developing EY practice as they arise will help increase your confidence and develop your professional knowledge, skills and expertise. Take your mind map plan to your ECT mentor review meetings. It will enable you to discuss your progress and seek advice from your mentor regarding how you can move forward with your professional development in your chosen area. Revisit your mind map in the light of discussion and suggestions from your mentor.

# Now what?

## Practical ways to implement this in the classroom

## Practical task for tomorrow

Audit your own subject knowledge across the EYFS, identifying areas for development within each of the ELGs. Use the statutory framework for the EYFS (DfE, 2021a) as a point of reference to enable you to pinpoint aspects within each ELG on which to focus. Consider your existing knowledge and next steps and avenues to explore which will increase your understanding. Table 2.1 provides an example which demonstrates how you might approach this task.

Table 2.1 Early years subject knowledge audit

| Prime or specific area of the EYFS (DfE, 2021a) | Early Learning Goal (DfE, 2021a) | Aspect of the ELG (DfE, 2021a) | My existing knowledge | My next steps | Avenues to explore (literature, visits, resources etc) |
|---|---|---|---|---|---|
| **Example:**<br><br>*Mathematics (Specific)* | *Number* | *'Children at the expected level of development will:*<br><br>*Subitise (recognise quantities without counting) up to 5'* (DfE, 2021a, p 14) | *Some understanding of the principle of subitising and what it means.*<br><br>*Some existing resources and activities in my repertoire.* | *Develop a greater understanding of why subitising is important to young children's mathematical development and future success.*<br><br>*Build a range of resources and activities that will support children to subitise numbers to 5.* | **Explore the following websites:**<br><br>• University of Cambridge Faculty of Mathematics (2022) NRICH: EY Subitising. [online] Available at: https://nrich.maths.org/public/topic.php?group_id=73&code=-794 (accessed 13 August 2022).<br><br>• Teach Starter (2022) Subitising Activities for Kids – The Importance of Teaching Subitising. [online] Available at: www.teachstarter.com/gb/blog/subitising-activities-for-kids-gb (accessed 13 August 2022).<br><br>**Read the following journal article:**<br><br>• Sayers, J, Andrews, P and Björklund Boistrup, L (2016) The Role of Conceptual Subitising in the Development of Foundational Number Sense. |

| Prime or specific area of the EYFS (DfE, 2021a) | Early Learning Goal (DfE, 2021a) | Aspect of the ELG (DfE, 2021a) | My existing knowledge | My next steps | Avenues to explore (literature, visits, resources etc) |
|---|---|---|---|---|---|
| Communication and Language | | | | | • Visit experienced colleague in the parallel class to observe focused activities and continuous provision opportunities to support subitising. |
| Physical Development | | | | | |
| Personal, Social and Emotional Development | | | | | |
| Literacy | | | | | |
| Mathematics | | | | | |
| Understanding the World | | | | | |
| Expressive Arts and Design | | | | | |

These areas of the EYFS curriculum focus may feed into your ECT reviews with your mentor or inspire you to create a more detailed professional development mind map, as we explored in the reflective task earlier in this chapter. Seeking opportunities to increase your EYFS curriculum knowledge, through visiting settings, accessing high-quality resources and liaising with relevant subject co-ordinators or EY colleagues, will help you to move forward in your journey as an EYT and EY expert.

## Practical task for next week ◀◀◀

### Your EYT assessment toolkit

A range of opportunities support you to gather information relating to the children you teach, such as observations, SST, focused activities and RBA. These could be referred to as your 'EYT assessment toolkit'. Your growing knowledge of these formative assessment strategies, the more formal RBA and the summative EYFSP at the end of the Reception year, supports you to consider the specific learning and development needs of the children in your class or as they transition to the next stage of their learning journey.

Reflect upon the varied assessment strategies that you use in your daily practice. Table 2.2 below will help you to reflect upon how each of these EY assessment opportunities can contribute to your growing knowledge of the children. You may think of further assessment strategies that you use in your setting, which you can add.

As you gather knowledge from various assessment opportunities, have discussions with your TA about how this information can be used, alongside your existing shared knowledge of the individual, to facilitate opportunities that will support progress. If you are working with pre-school-aged children, observations, anecdotal evidence and professional conversations will form the basis of assessment opportunities to support your understanding of the 'holistic' learning journey of the child.

## Practical task for the long term ◀◀◀

At the end of the academic year, take the time to read the new EYFS assessment and reporting arrangements (ARA). The Department for Education provides guidance which is updated annually and supersedes previous ARA publications. Securing this knowledge in advance can help you to consider and plan for the learning and assessment opportunities across the EYFS curriculum as you move into the new academic year.

Table 2.2 Early years assessment strategies

| Early years assessment opportunity | When does this happen? | Who is involved? | What can I learn? | How will it help me to support the learning and development of the child? | Next steps? |
|---|---|---|---|---|---|
| Transition – Home visit | Summer term prior to starting school | Parent/carer<br><br>EYT<br><br>TA | Dynamics of the family and relationships PSED (EYFS – prime area).<br><br>Child's interests and enthusiasms (CoETL).<br><br>Strengths and areas of development across EYFS.<br><br>Interactions with the child to gain knowledge of communication, language and understanding (EYFS prime area).<br><br>Observations of the child's physical development – both fine and gross motor control (EYFS prime area). | Better understanding of the pupil to support smooth transition and planning for learning opportunities that support the child to progress.<br><br>Any prime areas of learning that may need additional intervention or collaboration with the SENDCo. | Liaise with SENDCo.<br><br>Arrange parent/carer consultation to discuss settling-in period (late September).<br><br>Facilitate further opportunities to observe/assess prime area, eg speech.<br><br>Have further discussion with pre-school setting. |

| | | | |
|---|---|---|---|
| Induction – Stay and play sessions | | | |
| RBA | | | |
| Observations of play | | | |
| Focused activity | | | |
| Interactions with the child | | | |
| Examples of children's work | | | |
| Observation of child interacting with peers | | | |
| Discussions with parent/carer | | | |
| Transition meeting with previous setting | | | |
| Formative phonics assessment | | | |
| Formative maths assessment | | | |
| EYFS profile (end of Reception) | | | |
| Observations of the CoETL | | | |
| Other | | | |

# What next? ◀◀◀

## Further reading

Brodie, K (2013) *Observation, Assessment and Planning in the Early Years*. London: Open University Press.

Department for Education (DfE) (2021) *Reception Baseline Assessment and Reporting Arrangements*. London: Crown.

Dubiel, J (2016) *Effective Assessment in the Early Years Foundation Stage*. 2nd ed. London: Sage.

## References

Abrahamson, L (2018) *The Early Years Teacher's Book*. London: Sage.

Bottrill, G (2020) *School and the Magic of Children*. London: Sage.

Brodie, K (2014) *Sustained Shared Thinking in the Early Years*. London: Routledge.

Department for Education (DfE) (2011) *Teachers' Standards: Guidance for School Leaders, School Staff and Governing Bodies*. London: Crown.

Department for Education (DfE) (2021a) *Statutory Framework for the Early Years Foundation Stage*. London: Crown.

Department for Education (DfE) (2021b) *Development Matters: Non-statutory Curriculum Guidance for the Early Years Foundation Stage*. London: Crown.

Department for Education (DfE) (2021c) *Reception Baseline Assessment and Reporting Arrangements*. London: Crown.

Department for Education (DfE) (2022) *Early Years Foundation Stage Profile 2022 Handbook*. London: Crown.

Dubiel, J (2014) *Effective Assessment in the Early Years Foundation Stage*. London: Sage.

Fitzgerald, D and Kay, J (2016) *Understanding Early Years Policy*. London: Sage.

Little Learners (2020a) Understanding EAL. [online] Available at: www.youtube.com/watch?v=AiMP8z6s9Zk (accessed 13 August 2022).

Little Learners (2020b) Supporting EAL Learners. [online] Available at: www.youtube.com/watch?v=tv8mnnT1MwY (accessed 13 August 2022).

McDowall-Clark, R (2020) *Childhood in Society for the Early Years*. London: Sage.

Miller, L and Hevey, D (2012) *Policy Issues in the Early Years*. London: Sage.

Mistry, M and Sood, K (2020) *Meeting the Needs of Young Children with English as an Additional Language: Research Informed Practice*. Abingdon: Routledge.

National Association for EAL (NALDIC) (2022) [online] Available at: https://naldic.org.uk (accessed 13 August 2022).

Sargeant, M (2016) *100 Ideas for Early Years Practitioners: Supporting EAL Learners*. London: Bloomsbury.

Sayers, J, Andrews, P and Björklund Boistrup, L (2016) The Role of Conceptual Subitising in the Development of Foundational Number Sense. In Björklund Boistrup, L and Andrews, P (eds) *Mathematics Education in the Early Years* (pp 371–94). Cham: Springer.

Smidt, S (2015) *The Role of Observation and Assessment in Early Years Settings*. Oxon: Routledge.

Sylva, K, Melhuish, E, Sammons, P, Siraj-Blatchford, I and Taggart, B (2004) *The Effective Provision of Pre-School Education (EPPE) Project: Final Report: A Longitudinal Study Funded by the DfES 1997–2004*. London: Crown.

Teach Starter (2022) Subitising Activities for Kids: The Importance of Teaching Subitising. [online] Available at: www.teachstarter.com/gb/blog/subitising-activities-for-kids-gb/ (accessed 13 August 2022).

Tickell, C (2011) *The Early Years: Foundations for Life, Health and Learning: An Independent Report on the Early Years Foundation Stage to Her Majesty's Government*. London: Crown.

University of Cambridge, Faculty of Mathematics (2022) NRICH: EY Subitising. [online] Available at: https://nrich.maths.org/public/topic.php?group_id=73&code=-794 (accessed 13 August 2022).

Williams, L (2021) Little Learners in a Big World. In Pugh, V and Hughes, D (eds) *Teaching PSHE & R(S)E in Primary Schools: Enhancing the Whole Curriculum*. London: Bloomsbury.

# Chapter 3　The who, why and how of fostering effective relationships

# What? (The big idea)

## Relationships are key to effective early years teaching and learning

The relationships that you build will be key to effective teaching and learning as an early years (EY) early career teacher (ECT). Primarily this begins with you getting to know the children, establishing a secure and trusting rapport, fostering and modelling peer relationships and creating supportive routines. However, this cannot be done in isolation and as an early years teacher (EYT) you will be in a unique position as the first port of call for parents/carers as their child starts school. For any ECT this can be daunting, as well as a source of worry and anxiety. A great deal of effective communication with parents will need to be established – usually a triangulated approach between parent/carer, teacher, teaching assistant (TA) and the child. In addition, a child entering an EY setting may or may not yet have been identified with any additional needs. As an EY ECT you may need to work closely with your professional colleagues both in and beyond the school to support the development and needs of the children in your care. This chapter supports you to consider the multiple relationships that you need to establish to ensure progress for the children that you teach and your own professional success.

## Children at the heart of your practice

Consider a four or just-turned five year-old starting school or an even younger pre-schooler. Inevitably this tiny person will be full of mixed emotions. Some children take this big step in their stride, while for others it can be a bewildering, frightening and emotionally upsetting experience. For some children it may be the first experience of leaving their main carer. It will take time, compassion and care for the child to form an attachment to you as a significant adult in their life and their teacher. Personal, social and emotional development is an Early Years Foundation Stage (EYFS) prime area (DfE, 2021a) of learning and as such a cornerstone of building strong and effective relationships. As an EYT you are a role model with responsibilities as a 'parent by proxy'. The rapport that you establish in the early days of a child's induction is of paramount importance (Williams, 2021). Taking every opportunity to understand the child's journey so far, their family dynamic and getting to know the child's interests, needs and character can help you to settle a child and support the learning that will follow. Integral to your role is providing opportunities to facilitate children's purposeful interactions and relationships with the adults and their peers in the setting. This will support the child as they learn to effectively communicate, secure friendships, navigate and resolve conflicts, and build self-regulation strategies. You will play an influential part in the child blossoming as a unique individual who will carry them forward on their learning journey.

## Reflective task ◀◀◀

- How will you interact with the children to ensure that you maintain their eye contact and attention?

- How can you remain professional yet open with your body language and facial expressions?

- What age-appropriate language will you use to communicate in a clear and articulate manner?

- What parts of your week can be used to carve out time to get to know individual children in your class?

- Get down to the child's level when communicating.

- Never underestimate the power of a smile; show excitement, warmth and care.

- Break down instructions into bite-size steps.

- Your TA may be happy to take turns to read the class a story at the end of the school day, allowing you the opportunity to engage in one-to-one interaction.

## Developing parent/carer partnerships

Forging professional relationships with parents/carers can be a real source of anxiety for ECTs. In all honesty, even the most experienced teachers feel daunted when starting to get to know the parents of their new class. For you, there is the additional worry of *'Will they think I am inexperienced?'*, *'Will they take me seriously?'*, *'Will my role as their child's teacher be respected?'* All very valid fears for you. Rest assured, with mutually respectful communication paired with your interest and desire to make a difference to their child, these relationships will develop and flourish over time. As an EYT, this relationship and partnership is key to quickly settling the child into new routines, the success of the learning that follows, effective communication, and resolution of social and learning challenges as the child's year progresses. *'It is essential to seek out opportunities to forge meaningful and appropriate links with parents of the children in your class'* (Cremin and Burnett, 2018, p 500). Approaching and valuing every family with a genuine openness and respect, regardless of your own personal experience or cultural difference, is critically important (Sykes, 2016). Additionally, the unique and privileged position you have as often the first point of contact for families, as an ambassador for your school, can feel like an additional pressure and responsibility. But have confidence in yourself: there are practical ways in which these key relationships can be nurtured.

## Reflective task ◀◀◀

- How can you get to know the families prior to children starting your class?

- When in the school day can you be available to parents?

- If a parent/carer shares a concern, how will you respond?

- If you need to discuss something with a parent/carer, how will you approach them?

- Events such as home visits, induction meetings and 'stay and play' sessions are an effective way to begin to build relationships.

- The beginning and end of the school day can be a good time to be present and available.

- Listen and ensure that you follow up a parent/carer's concern (getting support from a senior member of staff, or your DSL if needed). A telephone call or catch up at the end of the school day will ensure the parent/carer feels listened to and supported.

- The playground may not be the most private space to initiate discussions, particularly when sensitive issues arise.

## Valuing and utilising your early years team

TAs are precious individuals in schools and learning communities, and the early years teaching assistant can be pure gold! Often their knowledge, experience, training and professional qualifications make them EY experts and they deserve to be valued as such. As an ECT, this close working relationship can be incredibly powerful in your initial journey as a teacher. When this relationship is nurtured and mutually respectful, children and their families benefit immensely. Parents and carers will feel secure in the knowledge that their child is in safe hands with a team of EY professionals. That they can turn to anyone in this team for support, help and guidance if needed. The far-reaching impact for the children will be seen, for example, in the way they enter their learning environment, where the adults model effective relationships. However, this does not just happen; it takes time, patience and respect (and a good measure of humour) to form a solid team with a shared EY vision and philosophy. An effective working partnership with your TA can also support opportunities for you to observe and assess the children while the TA takes the lead in focused activities under your guidance and planning. As in any setting or classroom, a TA's skills and time should be utilised and planned for effectively to benefit and scaffold the children's learning and development. Through collaboration and involvement in the planning and assessment process, the TA will be actively invested in teaching and learning to support pupil progress (Hewett, 2015). From a child's perspective, a strong bond can form with the TA who may be their key person and often as important as their class teacher.

## Reflective task ◀◀◀

- What ways can you involve your TA in planning?

- Get to know your TA – what are their educational and personal interests?

- Who is responsible for the 'menial jobs' around the classroom (eg paint pot washing, preparing displays, toileting accidents)?

- How will you build a happy EY team?

## Top tips ◀◀◀

- Your TA's contributions, extensive knowledge of the children, progress and the school systems can be invaluable information.

- Your TA's interests and specialist knowledge can be incorporated and utilised in the classroom.

- Work as a team and take turns in these tasks – after all, teamwork makes the dream work!

- Saying thank you and small tokens of appreciation go a long way.

### Working with other colleagues in school

Though every setting may be different, take time to understand the roles and responsibilities of the team and how they can support you to seek expert advice. These colleagues may range from the head, the deputy, phase/key stage leads, subject co-ordinators, the DSL, the Special Educational Needs and Disabilities Co-ordinator (SENDCo), administrative staff and TAs. Academy trusts will have management infrastructures in place across many schools and this can offer opportunities to work alongside colleagues in the same age range/phase as you. Your relationships with colleagues in school will form an incredibly important support network as you move through your ECT period. Initially this will inevitably be from those in your immediate work environment, such as teachers in parallel/ adjacent classes, the phase/key stage leader and TAs. This team of colleagues will liaise with planning, organisation, teaching and learning within the EY setting. Extending beyond this, staff that support the children in their day-to-day routines, such as lunchtime supervisors and before and after-school club staff, will also be important to your knowledge of the children and how they transition through their day. From a child's perspective, the adults who they encounter throughout the school day, from leaving their parent/carer in the morning until they are reunited at the close of the school day, should aim for seamless communication to ensure that the child feels safe and secure. As an ECT, your mentor will be a key person in your professional journey who you will work closely with to reflect upon your practice, identifying key areas of strength and development.

## Reflective task ◀◀◀

- When in the school day can you find opportunities to build effective communication with lunchtime supervisors and colleagues on playground duty?

- How will you establish early and continual dialogue with colleagues in the next phase of transition for the children you teach (eg pre-school to Reception, Reception to Year 1)?

- What ideas can you contribute to team meetings?

- How can you contribute as a team player to the wider life of the school?

## Top tips ◀◀◀

- These colleagues have essential information and perspectives on the children's social interactions and relationships during these times in the school day. This information can support you to understand the challenges that may follow them back into the classroom.

- These conversations will help you and your colleagues to plan and really know the children and their needs, smoothing later transitions.

- Colleagues will appreciate your fresh perspective, energy, input and enthusiasm!

- Being proactive and supportive will help you build connections within an established team and contribute to the wider life of the setting and school, eg volunteering to help with additional playground duties.

### Wider professional relationships beyond your setting

Your professional relationships will inevitably expand beyond the school you are working in. This will be important to your professional success in many aspects of your role. Seizing opportunities to share good EY practice with colleagues from other schools can be particularly beneficial if you are the only practitioner in a single-form setting. As teachers we are magpies, collecting ideas to enrich our practice. Building connections with other EYTs will provide a wealth of ideas to enhance provision, innovative teaching strategies and creative ways of working. Dialogue across schools surrounding planning, assessment and progress in the EYFS can enhance your knowledge, understanding and the professional judgements you make. Beyond your own school's EY setting, visiting nurseries and pre-schools in your locality can prove fruitful. Not only can this support you with transitions by meeting the children who will be entering your setting, but this can also allow you to liaise with staff to build a successful EY practitioner network.

Your developing knowledge of the children in your care may also require you to work with multi-agency professionals. A child entering an EY setting may or may not yet have been identified with additional needs. As an ECT you may be required to work closely with the SENDCo to identify, plan and deliver interventions in response to the developing child and their needs. Expert support may need to be put in place from a range of professionals (eg educational psychologists, speech and language therapists) who will assess the child's needs and offer expertise and strategies that you can put in place to facilitate learning. As an EYT, alongside a more senior school colleague, you may be required to attend multi-agency meetings. Multi-agency teams of professionals (which may include social workers, school nurses, family support workers, educational psychologists etc) work alongside school and parent/carer to provide services to support and meet the needs of the child's academic, personal, social and emotional development (Abrahamson, 2018).

## Reflective task ◀◀◀

- Who can be part of your supportive network beyond your school and immediate colleagues?

- What can you do to be proactive and expand your own EY knowledge and understanding, connections and build supportive networks?

- How will you utilise and act upon expert advice?

- What additional training or CPD will support your knowledge and understanding when working with individuals in your class?

## Top tips ◀◀◀

- Ask to visit a range of EY settings to increase your knowledge and understanding of EY pedagogy and practice.

- Join EY social media forums (eg blogs, vlogs, Twitter, Facebook, Instagram) and make connections with EY practitioners and teachers in the UK and further afield. Add to your bank of EY ideas and strategies for teaching and learning, behaviour management, display, classroom organisation and more.

- You cannot be an expert in all areas, but you can learn so much from other professionals (eg educational psychologist, school nurse, speech and language etc). Ask questions to increase your understanding and support the children in your care.

- Discuss with your mentor/SENDCo any additional training, CPD or visits to alternative/specialist settings that will support you to meet the needs of the children you are working with.

# So what?

## What difference does it make?

As an EYT you will need to gather information and evidence from a broad range of sources to build a holistic picture of the children you teach. Vital to this, in the first instance, is gleaning information from others who know the child well. These initial interactions will help you ascertain baseline information supporting you to settle the children and understand next steps in learning throughout the 17 EYFS areas of development (DfE, 2021a). Input from parents, colleagues in school or previous EY settings and multi-agency professionals all play a part in the information that is communicated.

Your own knowledge and understanding of the whole child will evolve over time, as you get to know the individual and their CoETL – playing and exploring; active learning; and creative and critical thinking (DfE, 2021b). Fundamentally, these characteristics empower EYTs to shine a light on how a child best learns and engages, what motivates them, how they solve problems and overcome challenges, how they interact with their environment and the relationships within it. Working closely with your TA and valuing their input is critical, since they too will have a wealth of knowledge and observations of each child and their progress over time, adding to this rich picture. Utilising their perspective and expertise, as well as the perspectives of other professionals and, importantly, parents/carers, will benefit you as the teacher to plan for, scaffold and facilitate the child's learning journey, supporting their emotional, social and academic progress in the EYFS and beyond.

Brookfield (1995) developed a reflective tool that encourages others, from a multiple perspective viewpoint, to reflect upon situations and events. These reflective lenses can be used to look at situations or events from multiple perspectives: the autobiographical lens – your own thoughts and feelings; the learners' lens – the event seen through the child's eyes; colleagues' lens – the perspective, thoughts and opinions of your professional colleagues; and the literature – what does the most current research and literature say? Hanson (2012, p 3) considered a fifth lens – the 'peripheral socio-cultural lens'. This lens requires a consideration of the impact of the social context or climate (external events like Covid-19, parent losing their job, your own personal circumstances) and how these factors influence the other reflective lenses. As an EYT, it is also important for you to consider the perceptive of parents/carers, particularly considering the importance of parental partnership in your daily practice. How can all these perspectives support you to make a well-rounded decision, judgement or conclusion in aspects of your practice?

## Reflective task ◀◀◀

Use Table 3.1 to consider an aspect of your EY practice and examine it through Brookfield's (1995) reflective lenses in the first instance, then from the parent/carers' perspective and finally through the socio-cultural lens (Hanson, 2012). To get you started with this reflective task you could consider any of the following aspects of your practice: the induction programme you offer; how your setting conducts home visits; the children's first day at school; morning and home-time routines; phonics, focused activities; continuous provision opportunities; or how your setting communicates the child's learning journey.

Table 3.1  Aspect of practice from different perspectives

| Aspect of practice: Reflect upon your chosen aspect of practice using Brookfield's (1995) four lenses. | |
| --- | --- |
| Lens 1: The autobiographical lens | |
| Lens 2: The learners' eyes | |
| Lens 3: Colleagues' eyes | |
| Lens 4: Literature | |
| | |
| Parent/carer lens | |
| | |

| ▶▶ | **Aspect of practice:** Reflect upon your chosen aspect of practice using Brookfield's (1995) four lenses. | |
|---|---|---|
| Consider the contributory factors in the social or cultural context or climate (Hanson, 2012): the socio-cultural lens | | |
| What has looking at this area of practice using all these different perspectives made you realise or consider? | | |
| Is there a particular lens that is most important to consider (above others)? Can you rank them from most to least important? | | |
| How might you adapt your practice in the light of these perspectives? | | |
| Is there support you need from others to develop this aspect of your practice? | | |
| Are there factors and reasons (within and beyond your control) why adaptations to your practice may be difficult to make? | Within your control: Beyond your control: | |
| How will you communicate this to children, children and colleagues? | Children: Parents: Colleagues: | |
| Has your own perspective (the autobiographical lens) on this aspect of your practice altered or developed because of reflection through the different lenses? | | |

## Case study ◀◀◀

The first weeks of induction had been smooth for Alex's new Reception class. The parents/carers had been bringing the children straight into the classroom and settling them before leaving the classroom. This had been effective because Alex and the TA could support any children who were feeling anxious and once the child was settled a phone call could be made to inform the parent/carer so that they could get on with their day in the knowledge that their child was happy and secure. Alex took the decision that Monday morning would be a suitable time to implement the new routine which was usual for all classes across the school – lining up on the playground at the start of the day. This was communicated to parents on Friday after school with a note to the parents/carers in bookbags.

Monday morning:

Teacher: *I feel confident that the children are now ready for the next step in their morning routine – saying goodbye to their parent/carer, lining up and organising their own belongings.*

Colleague *I worry that this next step is too soon. Some children can feel wobbly after being at home with family over the weekend. Changing routine on a Monday morning may be confusing for the children and families. Perhaps slowly putting the new routine in place over the course of the week would be better.*

Parent/carer: *Why is everyone on the playground? Have I missed something? My child is upset and clinging to me. I have just learnt from another parent that the routine is changing from today. Apparently, there was a note in the bookbag but I must have missed it.*

Child: *I want my daddy to take me into my classroom so I can play with the building blocks with him for a little bit, like he usually does. I feel scared and sad standing on my own. I don't want to go into my classroom alone; I want to go home with daddy.*

Despite going out onto the playground early to receive the children, Alex can already see the difficulty with this swift change in routine. Some of the adults look nervous and there are some children that are clinging to their parents/carers. Alex decides to reflect in the moment. Realising that this big step is too soon, she suggests that parents/carers line up with their children and walk them around to the classroom with their belongings.

## Reflective task ◀◀◀

- How could Alex have mitigated this chain of events?

- Who should have been involved in discussions prior to changing the routine?

- How could these discussions support Alex with decisions about how and when to change the morning routine?

- What could Alex have done to communicate more effectively with parents/carers?

- What should Alex do next to ensure that Tuesday morning runs smoothly for the children and their families?

- What steps should Alex take next to ensure the new lining-up routine is successfully in place by the end of the week?

# Now what?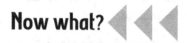

## Practical ways to implement this in the classroom

### Practical task for tomorrow ◀◀◀

When you are out with your TA on the playground in the morning, reflect upon the following questions.

- How can you create a welcoming atmosphere?

- What interactions will you have with the children?

- What can you do to ensure you are approachable to parents/carers?

- How will you approach parents/carers?

- How will you open dialogue about their child?

These anecdotal conversations will support you and your TA to get to know the children and families, supporting your ability to understand the child and their next steps. This will also help you to see things with fresh eyes.

### Practical task for next week ◀◀◀

Invite the parents/carers of children with specific needs into school to discuss their child's needs. This could be personal, social and emotional, medical, communication, physical needs, EAL or identified SEND. The conversation you facilitate will help you to see the child through the parent/carers' eyes. This can be highly informative in assisting you to understand the child's learning journey so far and how you can support moving forward. You may wish to seek the support of your SENDCo or phase lead for those children with identified or possible unidentified SEND or for sensitive issues that arise. The questions in Table 3.2 may help you to frame and scaffold this meeting.

**Table 3.2 Parent/carer meeting questions**

| Getting to know the child... | Tell me about your child... |
|---|---|
| (Breaking the ice and building rapport is important. The parent/carer needs to feel that they are not being judged and that you wish to build a genuine connection with them and their child.) | What are your child's interests?<br><br>Does your child have a favourite toy or activity?<br><br>Does your child already know anyone else in the setting?<br><br>How does your child interact with others? Does your child have a best friend?<br><br>How does your child play and learn best at home?<br><br>What are your child's strengths?<br><br>Is there anything that your child finds tricky? |
| **Understanding family dynamics...**<br><br>(This can be a sensitive area of enquiry, particularly if the family dynamics are complex. By focusing the questions on the child and family life in a non-judgemental way parents will usually volunteer information.) | **Tell me about your family...**<br><br>Does your child have siblings? Are they younger or older?<br><br>How does your child interact with their sibling(s)?<br><br>Who lives in the household?<br><br>Are there any family pets in the household?<br><br>For EAL children:<br><br>What is the first language spoken at home?<br><br>Does your child understand/communicate in English and/or their first language?<br><br>What language do immediate family members understand/communicate in?<br><br>Are there family members who will need a translator when communicating with school?<br><br>How do you feel we can we best support your child to settle/build relationships/learn? |

| Understanding specific needs... | Tell me about your child's learning journey so far... |
|---|---|
| (This can be a particularly useful line of enquiry for children already identified SEND and those with possible unidentified needs.) | The questions in the first section 'Getting to know the child' will provide helpful initial insights.<br><br>Who has supported you and your child on their journey so far?<br><br>How did your child get the help they needed/ diagnosis?<br><br>When did your child have this support/ diagnosis?<br><br>Are there any areas that we can support with at school to help your child settle/build relationships/learn?<br><br>What strategies or routines work well for your child at home? |
| Parents/carers as partners in the child's learning journey... | How does your child feel about school/ friendships/learning?<br><br>What does your child tell you about school?<br><br>What do they enjoy at school?<br><br>What do they not enjoy about school?<br><br>How can we best support your child as they settle into school?<br><br>Do you have any concerns or worries that you would like to discuss?<br><br>Are there areas where we can support you by providing more information? |

## Practical task for the long term

Consider how you can utilise pupil and parent/carer voice to support the induction/transition process. Simple strategies such as a parent/carer questionnaire can support you to develop your practice and support future planning with their perspective in mind.

- What questions could be included on your questionnaire to further support your understanding and give you information to help you improve your induction/ transition process?

- How will you close the loop and communicate how you have used the information in future decisions about the induction/transition process?

With this new knowledge, consider the following questions to support any future actions you take.

- What changes would you like to implement as part of this process?

- Who may you need to consult prior to making changes?

- How will you communicate these changes to the parents/carers of your new cohort?

Capturing pupil voice can also support you to develop aspects of your practice and your EY curriculum.

- How will you capture this in a child-friendly way?

You could consider facilitating reflective circle times where pupils think about their magic moments. This can be an effective and child-friendly way to gather this information.

# What next?

## Further reading

Ward, U (2013) *Working with Parents in Early Years Settings*. 2nd ed. Los Angeles: Learning Matters.

Wilson, T (2018) *How to Develop Partnerships with Parents: A Practical Guide for the Early Years*. London: Routledge.

# References

Abrahamson, L (2018) *The Early Years Teacher's Handbook*. 2nd ed. London: Sage.

Brookfield, S (1995) *Becoming a Critically Reflective Teacher*. San Francisco, CA: Jossey-Bass.

Cremin, T and Burnett, C (2018) *Learning to Teach in the Primary School*. 4th ed. London: Routledge.

Department for Education (DfE) (2021a) *Statutory Framework for the Early Years Foundation Stage*. London: Department for Education.

Department for Education (DfE) (2021b) *Development Matters*. London: Department for Education.

Hanson, K J (2012) *How Can I Support Early Childhood Studies Undergraduate Students to Develop Reflective Dispositions?* EdD thesis, Exeter University.

Hewett, D (2015) *Innovative Teaching and Learning in Primary Schools*. London: Sage.

Sykes, G (2016) You as Partner in the Lives of Children, Families and Communities. In Cox, A and Sykes, G (eds) *The Multiple Identities of a Reception Teacher*. Los Angeles: Learning Matters.

Williams, L (2021) Little Learners in a Big World. In Pugh, V and Hughes, D (eds) *Teaching PSHE & R(S)E in Primary Schools: Enhancing the Whole Curriculum*. London: Bloomsbury.

# Chapter 4 How to create a successful enabling learning environment

## What? (The big idea) ◀◀◀

### The early years juggling act

This chapter promotes consideration of the important concept of the enabling learning environment as *'the third teacher'*, as touched upon in Chapter 1: 'What is it like to be an early years teacher?' As an early career teacher (ECT) in early years (EY) settings you may find the *'juggling act'* of facilitating the Early Years Foundation Stage (EYFS) curriculum with its 17 areas of learning a challenge. The balance of child-led and adult-led focused activities within the continuous provision are integral to this, as well as rejuvenating the enabling learning environment to keep it fresh and appealing – igniting a sense of curiosity, awe and wonder for the children while providing opportunities that stretch and challenge. This chapter considers how you can plan and provide the resources necessary for effective continuous provision while skilfully managing the learning environment. It will consider how your choice of resources can affect the role and the value of enhanced continuous provision in the classroom, while striving for a balance between child-led and adult-led focused activities. It reflects upon the use of indoor and outdoor provision; the impact this can have on a child's development and how you can encourage children to become independent learners through the opportunities you facilitate.

## Managing the enabling environment

The importance of the learning environment as a key principle in enabling children to learn is considered in the statutory framework for EYFS (DfE, 2021). Primarily, an enabling learning environment should be seen as so much more than the physical space that you provide in your classroom. Creating a welcoming, safe place where children feel valued and cared for is imperative for them to thrive. Positive relationships are a key factor, not only within the EY team, but also in the way in which you will respect and value parents and carers as an integral part of their child's learning journey. For the children, this enabling learning environment should encourage social skills, for example, collaboration – where peer relationships can flourish through play opportunities and activities that meet a diverse range of needs. The inclusive nature of the EY learning environment that you create will be of upmost importance, entitling every 'unique child' to be valued and included regardless of any additional needs or their socio-cultural background. Borkett (2018, p 15) describes how a whole-team approach is fundamental to 'truly inclusive practice' where views, ideals and situations can be openly discussed. Your role as an early years teacher (EYT) is to be professionally curious about the children as 'unique' individuals. What experiences do they bring with them? What are their interests? How do they learn best? Do they prefer learning in the indoor or outdoor classroom? What are their next steps? What are their individual needs, strengths and areas for development? You will use this growing knowledge to build opportunities into the way you plan your enabling learning environment both indoors and outdoors. The range of activities and resources available should promote opportunities for exploration, igniting imagination, problem solving and moments where children can reflect across all areas of the EYFS curriculum. The EYFS (DfE, 2021) is described as a 'framework' rather than a 'curriculum', and as such does not stipulate a precise way to be implemented. Instead, this guidance provides EY practitioners with autonomy to plan in a way that meets the needs and next steps of the children in their care. So as an EYT where do you begin? It may be useful to think of the physical space, both indoors and outdoors, in terms of zones or activity areas, eg mathematical area, writing area, reading area, role play, construction, inquiry area, creative area etc. Burnham (2016) suggests looking at your learning environment through a child's eye and ensuring clear labelling and accessibility of resources and learning zones. Clearly labelled resources and areas provide opportunities for children to observe print in the environment, regardless of their reading ability, which can be used alongside pictures and numerals to demarcate the number of children permitted in the area at any one time. The physical space you design, utilising both the indoor and outdoor classroom, should also be viewed as a mental space, creating opportunities for young learners to work through and resolve problems which are conducive to their development as independent and resilient lifelong learners. The safety of the children in your care and risk management can be an additional pressure for you as an ECT. With responsibility for both indoor and outdoor learning environments this will be a key consideration, ensuring that equipment and spaces are maintained and well organised. You will also need to feel confident that the children are kept safe while giving ample explorative opportunities that permit them to take measured risks so that they can learn to be responsible. Your behaviour management strategies such as co-constructing 'safe play rules' with the children will support them to see potential risks and the measures that they can put in place to safely manage themselves and be mindful of others.

## Reflective task ◀◀◀

- How will you manage the space and areas of learning in your indoor and outdoor learning environment?

- Who will be responsible for maintenance and organisation of these spaces?

- How frequently will you change or update areas or zones in your enabling learning environment both indoors and outdoors?

- How can the existing provision be enhanced or updated?

## Top tips ◀◀◀

- As an EY team, plan together and devise an overview of what you need each week in the continuous provision both indoors and outdoors.

- Assign children as monitors to be responsible for tidying and organising areas of the enabling learning environment, eg the writing area. Change these monitor roles regularly so that children see the learning environment as a shared responsibility.

- Consider the immersive learning environment by planning an overarching topic or theme, eg think about the role play area over a four- to six-week period, rather than changing weekly. Add resources that enhance and refresh the existing provision. An 'Under the Sea' role play area could have resources added such as non-fiction books, reference materials and magnifying glasses as the topic progresses.

- Alternatively, consider 'deconstructed role play' – where resources are portable, multi-functional and the purpose is not specified, eg tablecloths, napkins and other utensils. This can ignite imaginative role play opportunities for the children to explore with the autonomy to choose where they play, in the indoor or outdoor learning environment.

## Choices, challenges and contentions

Borkett (2018) conveys that there may be times when providing an enabling environment can be difficult to achieve due to a lack of continued professional development for you and staff working in EY settings. Challenges could also extend to wider school expectations, lack of funding and resources, as well your confidence surrounding the ever-changing and evolving policy in the field of EY. A further contention that can heavily impact upon your EY practice and the children's learning experience is making informed decisions about how you will approach and plan the continuous provision within your setting. Depending on how established the practice is in the setting and team in which you are working, your role as an EY ECT may hold varying degrees of decision making about the planning, design and implementation of the enabling learning environment. More recent EY schools of thought surround skills-based approaches to the continuous provision. Bottrill (2018) contends that EYTs must be mindful that provision reflects the child's voice and interests, which may mean steering away from adult-led thematic approaches. Balancing the demands that you as an EYT may feel to provide evidence of outcomes against each ELG while prioritising the discovery and exploration that every child has a right to can be challenging. However, it is acknowledged that there may be times when a topic or theme-based approach to continuous provision may be desirable to fully immerse children in cross-curricular learning, particularly if a desire to learn more in a particular area has been expressed by the children. Williams (2020, p 131) describes planning for purposeful child-led opportunities as the 'continuous provision conundrum', which is particularly challenging for those inexperienced or new to teaching in EY settings. For you as an EY ECT, making continuous provision decisions will inevitably be more meaningful when you know the children well and cater for their next steps to ensure progress and independence in their skills application to cement deep learning. A hybrid approach combining skills development alongside some thematic continuous provision, which encompasses the learners' interests, may afford you and the children the best of both worlds. This way you will be planning for open-ended exploration as well as some immersive and interconnected thematic opportunities, while providing purposeful and meaningful scope to rehearse and develop key skills.

## Reflective task ◀◀◀

- Reflecting on your existing practice, what approach does your setting currently adopt and what are the positive aspects and limitations?

- How will you build the child's voice into your planning for continuous provision?

- How will you ensure that the enabling environment provides opportunities for children to develop skills?

- Reflecting on your existing practice, are there benefits from a thematic or topic-based approach to the continuous provision for some aspects of practice?

## Top tips ◀◀◀

- Plan as a team for the continuous provision within your enabling learning environment. It is a time- and labour-intensive aspect of EY practice which runs more smoothly if there is a shared consensus and responsibility.

- Walk children through the setting as part of your ongoing practice and have purposeful interactions about their areas of interest or what could be added to different zones or areas, such as a construction area, sand, water etc.

- Consider what skills have been a focus for your weekly planning and how these can be incorporated into the continuous provision through the challenges and activities you provide, eg printing words with key phonics learnt in the creative area.

- If you are uncertain about incorporating a thematic or topic-related approach, focus on the skills that you want the children to develop and keep these at the heart of your practice, eg developing your role play area to reflect a familiar tale may offer immersion through story retelling and purposeful opportunities for language development and writing skills.

### The importance of play in the planning cycle

When discussing the importance of 'child-led learning' and continuous provision in the enabling learning environment, you cannot escape how this brings you back to the concept of play. Even 'adult-led focused' activities can be planned to include playful opportunities. Earlier in Chapter 1: 'What is it like to be an early years teacher?' you were encouraged to toy with the notion of play, establishing your own thoughts and philosophy to empower you to challenge how others may perceive play in the EY, particularly play and its importance to child development. It will frame the decisions you make about play opportunities in the continuous provision which promote progress in the children's learning journey across the holistic EY curriculum.

> The overall aim in any early years setting should be to make sure that ALL children make progress in ALL areas of learning and development, whilst having fun, being happy and developing skills for life. To ensure this progression it is important to follow an ongoing cycle of planning in which the importance of play, assessment and review play an equal part.
>
> (Beeley, 2016, p 8)

**Figure 4.1 The cycle of planning for play (based on Beeley, 2016)**

Beeley (2016) discusses how the '*planning for play*' approach should be seen as a complete cycle for children to make progress through the '*plan, play, assess, review*' continuum (Figure 4.1). The way in which the enabling learning environment continually develops and evolves is a result of what you will do in response to the individual children. Planning for play requires the children to lead and you as their EYT to join them on their journey. This approach focuses less on you planning activities, but rather on a distinct shift to planning the physical learning environment to promote choice and independence. Your setting's learning environment needs to be designed in a way that promotes curiosity, creativity and stimulation through open-ended resources, which allow children to build their knowledge, skills and understanding in ways that are meaningful to them. Planning for play also considers the '*continuous provision conundrum*' that your attention was drawn to earlier in this chapter. It acknowledges that children's interest may be piqued through project or topic-based learning. Seminal work such as Piaget's theory on schema (1936) also considers how making meaningful learning connections can help children make sense of the world around them. As an EYT you can facilitate and plan for opportunities to extend the child's area of interest and take their project forward through posing questions, promoting discussion and challenging thoughts and ideas through 'sustained shared thinking'. As an EYT you will continually be reflecting on the play you observe to provide the next steps and facilitate learning. To ensure that resources in the continuous provision and adult-led activities are stimulating, you need to constantly reflect on the effectiveness of your planned enabling learning environment (McEvoy and McMahon, 2019).

## Reflective task ◀◀◀

- How will you incorporate the 'plan, play, assess, review' cycle into your daily practice?

- Reflecting on your existing practice, when have adult-led activities been useful?

- How will you ensure that the balance of child-led and adult-led activities is harmonious in your setting?

- From your training and ongoing CPD, what other learning and child development theories underpin learning through play?

## Top tips ◀◀◀

- It is key that you regard play as a window of opportunity to see children's independent application of knowledge and understanding.

- There will be times in your practice when more specific planned adult-led focused activities will be important, eg setting up opportunities and working with individuals to ascertain phonic or numerical knowledge and application or intervening to support and scaffold key learning before moving forward to ensure foundational knowledge is secure.

- Remember that your evidence in the children's learning journeys will need to reflect a balance of what the children can do in child-initiated and adult-led contexts.

- Having a solid understanding of the learning theory that underpins play and learning will be crucial in your justification of how you plan for play within the enabling environment.

## In-the-moment planning

Planning in the moment is a nuanced skill which will take time for you to master. It is about being responsive to the learner every time you listen, observe or interact. The principle of 'in-the-moment planning' revolves around the notion that children are most engaged and learn best when they are pursuing their own curiosities and interests (Ephgrave, 2020). In-the-moment planning is integrally linked to your everyday formative assessment and building a picture from the many puzzle pieces that you will acquire about the unique individual over time. This knowledge is then used to plan or momentarily add to the children's play and learning experience to extend enquiry and encourage development. A cornerstone of its success is your excellent rapport and knowledge of the children, who need to feel confident and safe within the enabling learning environment and with the adults working with them. As Ephgrave (2018, p 91) explains, 'deep level involvement indicates brain activity and progress' if children have good levels of well-being. Unlike more traditional planning where you would know in advance exactly where you intended learning to go, 'in-the-moment planning' encourages EYTs to play and interact with the children and spontaneously respond through being led by the children. In your enabling learning environment, you should provide open-ended 'loose parts' resources that offer a multitude of child-initiated play opportunities (Watkins, 2022). Choosing open-ended and versatile resources such as cardboard boxes, tubes and tyres can appeal to the child regardless of their topical interests and allow room for creativity, innovation and imagination. Regularly assessing your learning environment to see which areas and resources are effective in keeping children engaged and actively exploring can help you to consider how you will develop the enabling learning environment further. This may also allow opportunities to explore planning with the children so that they can express their ideas about how the area can be enhanced to meet their needs and interests.

## Reflective task ◀◀◀

- Reflecting on your experience, what resources may support 'in-the-moment planning'?

- When and how will you assess the effectiveness of the enabling learning environment?

- How will you record 'in-the-moment planning' opportunities in your weekly planning?

- How will you communicate the vision and philosophy of 'in-the-moment planning' with parents/carers?

## Top tips ◀◀◀

- Resources that are open-ended do not require a huge budget but will need replacing often. Create a list of such donatable resources and include these in your school or EY setting newsletter when needed.

- Looking at your enabling learning environment with a critical lens will help you to continually assess its effectiveness. Carve out time to observe the children in their child-led exploration of the spaces you provide and consider how you can develop, enhance or remaster areas to promote deeper engagement and exploration.

- Planning will inevitably look different when adopting an 'in-the-moment planning' approach. Your plans may need to evolve over the course of the day/week/term in response to the children's needs and interests.

- When adopting an 'in-the-moment planning' approach, you will inevitably need to establish a shared values approach among your team. However, it is equally important that parents/carers understand how this approach works. Share your practice about the 'in-the-moment planning' through 'stay and play' sessions or through the children's electronic or paper-based learning journals.

# So what? ◀ ◀ ◀

## What difference does it make?

High-quality planning is a cornerstone of your excellent EY practice. As an EYT you will be continually reflecting upon the opportunities that you are providing to the children to enhance the continuous provision and ensure skills progression. To support you to do this you will need to revisit your planning frequently. This may be 'in the moment' or over the course of the day, week or term. Now select an example of your own planning to reflect upon. This could be one of your weekly overviews of key learning intentions and skills that the children will be exploring.

Your overview could include:

» key learning intentions;

» a focus on skills;

» the prime and specific ELGs;

» whole-class teaching;

» focused activities;

» continuous provision opportunities (within the indoor and outdoor environment).

The case study and learning environment map (Figure 4.2) will support you to reflect on your own planning and consider the design of the continuous provision in the enabling learning environment.

## Case study ◀ ◀ ◀

Lori's Reception class has been retelling the story of *The Little Red Hen* this half term. This story raised lots of interesting questions for the children:

- How did the little red hen transport so much flour on her own?

- How does a mill work?

- How is bread made?

- What is corn?

- How does it become flour?

Over the course of the sequence of learning, Lori involved the children in planning the areas of learning environment so that she could facilitate and extend their knowledge and understanding. Each week Lori would revisit the plan that the children had created and use this to prompt discussion about their learning journey. Over time, Lori noticed that the children became experts in looking at the enabling learning environment and finding solutions and suggestions for what they would like to do next in each of the learning areas. The children even went home and found useful resources to add to and extend the continuous provision. As a team, the adults facilitated the children's requests by providing relevant resources in the learning environment. While the children were immersed in their play, the adults would interact with them to extend their thinking. Lori's favourite place to interact was in the role play area, where she would act in the role of the unhelpful dog or cat! Lori found that planning and facilitating play in this way resulted in the children being actively immersed in the story through retelling and problem-solving challenges. Lori presented these activities as 'optional' challenges for the children to solve. This flexibility allowed choice for all children; those that found learning in this interconnected way meaningful explored these challenges with gusto, whereas others could have the freedom to be more open-ended in the way in which they explored their learning environment. Lori found that the children's suggestions could naturally support the key learning intentions and skills that she as the teacher wanted the children to master. Examples of activities that evolved included a role play area, prop box outside and small world where children could re-enact the story using key vocabulary which supported language and communication development skills; areas in the indoor and outdoor space where children could weigh bags of flour or use the construction to create a vehicle to transport grain to the mill underpinned mathematical development, problem solving and personal social and emotional skills. Lori added new ideas to the class learning environment plan and detailed the skills and learning intentions in her own planning. These two plans together illustrated how the children's skills, understanding and knowledge developed throughout *The Little Red Hen* sequence of learning across the ELGs.

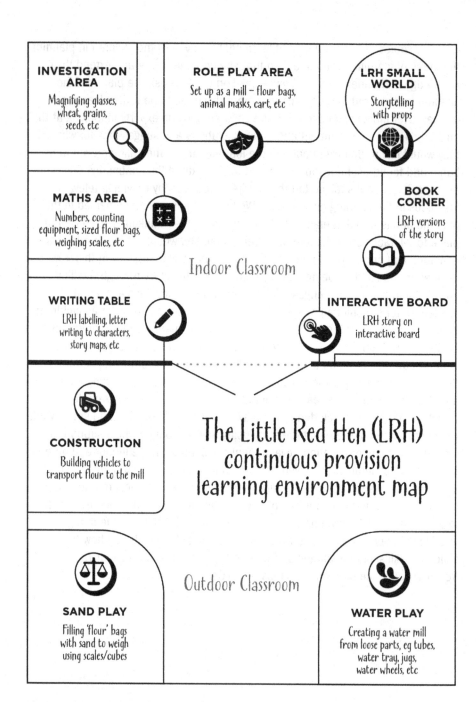

**INVESTIGATION AREA**

Magnifying glasses, wheat, grains, seeds, etc

**ROLE PLAY AREA**

Set up as a mill – flour bags, animal masks, cart, etc

**LRH SMALL WORLD**

Storytelling with props

**MATHS AREA**

Numbers, counting equipment, sized flour bags, weighing scales, etc

**BOOK CORNER**

LRH versions of the story

Indoor Classroom

**WRITING TABLE**

LRH labelling, letter writing to characters, story maps, etc

**INTERACTIVE BOARD**

LRH story on interactive board

**CONSTRUCTION**

Building vehicles to transport flour to the mill

The Little Red Hen (LRH) continuous provision learning environment map

**SAND PLAY**

Filling 'flour' bags with sand to weigh using scales/cubes

Outdoor Classroom

**WATER PLAY**

Creating a water mill from loose parts, eg tubes, water tray, jugs, water wheels, etc

**Figure 4.2  Learning environment map**

Having looked at the case study and learning environment map in Figure 4.2, revisit your planning overview and develop this into a practical map of your classroom, demonstrating where continuous provision will support the ELGs. Reflect upon your overview to consider the balance of child-led and adult-led focused activities on offer in your enabling learning environment. The following questions will help you to frame your reflections.

- Are there any areas that need developing or enhancing?

- When could you incorporate the child's voice?

- How will you ensure that the children's skills are developed?

- How will you balance child-led and adult-focused activities?

- How will you ensure that children are provided with child-initiated play opportunities?

- What will the role of the adults be?

# Now what?

## Practical ways to implement this in the classroom

Think about the opportunities you will design in the continuous provision to support children's development of skills and rehearsal of key learning objectives this week. The resources you use do not need to be expensive or elaborate – often open-ended resources are best since they can be used for a range of purposes. Audit the existing resources available in your enabling learning environment. Which of these resources are open-ended and can be used to support this key learning intention? Begin to think about how the resources and activities offered in the continuous provision support learning across the ELGs. Are there natural links with other areas of learning covered over the day/week/term? Now consider how you can extend the activity to offer challenge and keep it engaging. Use the rubric in Table 4.1 to begin to plan how these resources can be used to provide opportunities for

**Table 4.1 Auditing resources in the learning environment**

| Key learning intention | Resources | Where in the enabling learning environment? | Links to other ELGs and learning | Extending play | Organisation – resource management |
|---|---|---|---|---|---|
| ELG: Physical development – Fine Motor Control – develop fine motor control | Pine cones, seeds, different leaves from trees, tweezers | Tuff spot – outside under the rain shelter | Physical Development – ELG: Fine Motor Control<br><br>Understanding the World – ELG: The Natural World (links to science/Forest School – identifying trees) | Add pots with different-sized openings to extend the children's fine motor control and accuracy.<br><br>Challenge the children's knowledge of trees by labelling pots with pictures of trees and names. | Children asked to collect natural resources to replace those which are damaged/lost.<br><br>Monitors to tidy ensure tweezers and sorting pots with labels are in place each day. |
|  |  |  |  |  |  |
|  |  |  |  |  |  |

children to rehearse key skills through play. The example in Table 4.1 will support you to think about auditing and managing your own resources and how they can be used to support a variety of playful learning opportunities.

## Practical task for next week ◀◀◀

Finding out about the children's interests as they arise as a result of their learning experiences can provide incredible insight into what to provide in the continuous provision the following week. Children can be insightful and helpful with planning, so utilise their brilliant ideas. Talk to the children about their areas of interest and see how this can be built into your weekly continuous provision overview. This could be managed by allowing time at the end of the week for the children to reflect and think about where they would like their learning to take them next week. As an EYT you can scaffold this planning by asking the children to think about particular areas or zones within the enabling learning environment. Once you have gathered the children's ideas, you can then consider how different resources and opportunities in the various areas of the enabling learning environment (eg creative area, sand and water, role play etc) can support children to progress in their learning journey. Table 4.2 overleaf provides an example of how you might approach this task with the children and space for you to reflect on other examples from your own practice.

## Practical task for the long term ◀◀◀

As you complete the final term of the academic year, consider creating a long-term overview plan for the new academic year ahead. Reflect upon what has worked well and plot an overview of the next academic year which can be added to and adapted in response to your new cohort's needs and interests. Review how and where such adaptations can take place. There will have been many successes that you will incorporate into future planning. Equally there will be adjustments that you will wish to make to your practice, planning and the enabling learning environment as you get to know your new cohort of children, their interests and needs. This is a great time to get ahead as a team – tidying, sorting, organising and auditing resources. You may have a wish list of resources that need replacing or key items that will be invaluable for future provision. Sourcing materials does not need to be expensive. Being organised means that you can create a donation list or collect items in the natural environment to use in your learning environment. Look through the child's lens and ask the children what they have loved most about their learning environment as it has developed through the academic year – after all, their voice is so important.

Table 4.2 Planning from the children's interests and ideas

| Area of the classroom | Children's ideas | Links to areas of interest | Children's questions | Links to ELGs | Resources | Role of the adult |
|---|---|---|---|---|---|---|
| Investigation station | Flying kites<br>Making kites | Weather and wind power | How do kites fly?<br><br>What is the best material to make a kite from?<br><br>What shape kites fly the best? | Expressive Arts and Design – ELG: Creating with Materials<br><br>Understanding the World – ELG: The Natural World<br><br>Physical development – ELG: Fine Motor Skills<br><br>Communication and Language – ELG: Speaking | String<br>Material<br>Straws<br>Sticks<br>Glue<br>Scissors<br>Tape<br>Ribbon<br>Variety of real kites | Supporting making where needed.<br>Discussion about resources chosen.<br>Key questions to extend/challenge:<br>• How will your kite work?<br>• Why did you choose this material?<br>• How do you know this is the best material?<br>• How will you prove it can fly?<br>• What could you do to improve your kite? |
| Role play | | | | | | |
| Construction | | | | | | |
| Sand and water | | | | | | |
| Writing area | | | | | | |
| Maths area | | | | | | |
| Small world | | | | | | |
| Other | | | | | | |

# What next? ◀ ◀ ◀

## Further reading

Ephgrave, A (2018) *Planning in the Moment with Young Children*. Abingdon: Routledge.

McEvoy, J and McMahon, S (2019) *Child Centred Planning in the Early Years Foundation Stage*. London: Sage.

Watkins, S (2022) *Outdoor Play for Healthy Little Minds*. Abingdon: Routledge.

White, J (2020) *Playing and Learning Outdoors: The Practical Guide and Sourcebook for Excellence in Outdoor Provision and Practice with Young Children*. 3rd ed. Abingdon: Routledge.

## References

Beeley, K (2016) *Planning for Play: Child Led Inquiry in Early Years*. Dagenham: Playing to Learn.

Borkett, P (2018) *Cultural Diversity and Inclusion in Early Years Education*. London: Routledge.

Bottrill, G (2018) *Can I Go and Play Now?* London: Sage.

Burnham, L (2016) *How to be an Outstanding Early Years Practitioner*. London: Bloomsbury.

Department for Education (DfE) (2021) *Statutory Framework for the Early Years Foundation Stage*. London: Department for Education.

Ephgrave, A (2018) *Planning in the Moment with Young Children*. Abingdon: Routledge.

Ephgrave, A (2020) *Planning in the Moment with Two and Three Year Olds*. London: Routledge.

McEvoy, J and McMahon, S (2019) *Child Centred Planning in the Early Years Foundation Stage*. London: Sage.

Piaget, J (1936) *Origins of Intelligence in the Child*. London: Routledge & Kegan Paul.

Watkins, S (2022) *Outdoor Play for Healthy Little Minds*. Abingdon: Routledge.

Williams, L (2020) The Continuous Provision Conundrum – Quality Provision that Encapsulates the Child's Voice. In Carroll, J and Alexander, G (eds) *The Teachers' Standards in Primary Schools: Understanding and Evidencing Effective Practice*. London: Sage.

# Chapter 5 Where will the journey lead? Supporting children as unique individuals

# What? (The big idea)

### Hidden treasure

This chapter considers how early years teachers (EYTs) unlock potential in each 'unique child' to support them on their learning and developmental journey throughout the Early Years Foundation Stage (EYFS) and beyond. Earlier in Chapter 2: 'How to promote outstanding provision and purposeful assessment', you considered how the nationally recognised Reception Baseline Assessment (RBA) supports you as an EYT to gain an initial understanding of each child entering Reception. The Standards and Testing Agency's *Reception Baseline Assessment and Reporting Arrangements* (2021, p 5) state that the '*RBA will be used to create school-level progress measures for primary schools which will show the progress pupils make from reception until the end of key stage 2*'. This has implications for you as an EY ECT, as well as colleagues in Key Stages 1 and 2, and wider ramifications for the school. Yet, of fundamental importance is the anecdotal evidence that you gather over time that provides a full and rich picture of each child and their progressive journey. It is in finding the 'hidden treasure', valuing and nurturing every child's individuality and unique gifts, that you will be able to support every little gem to shine. This chapter will encourage you to contemplate the concept of 'school readiness' and how adapting practice and pedagogy can support transitions at each phase of the EY journey. Your expert knowledge of each unique individual will enable you to plan for learner progress at their own pace, as well as early identification of needs to provide timely strategic intervention where required. Your knowledge and support of the learner's progress over time, with a clear focus on learning and development, will build strong foundations for the learning that follows as they move through their primary school career and beyond.

## Each unique treasure trove

The *unique child* is an integral principle which guides EYFS practice. It is based upon the premise that '*every child is a unique child, who is constantly learning and can be resilient, capable, confident and self-assured*' (DfE, 2021a, p 6). But how did this term and definition come about? Why is it so vitally important to understand its origins and what it means to you as an EYT and the children that you will teach? Early theorists such as Freud, Rousseau and Froebel (cited in MacBlain, 2022) valued the uniqueness of each child, recognising emotional development as a central component of a child's learning and developmental experience. Not every child will begin their lives on an equal footing and inevitably such inequalities may significantly impact opportunities, learning and development. Ofsted (2019, p 31) acknowledge that children begin EY settings with differing learning and play experiences, contending that '*cultural capital is the essential knowledge that children need to prepare them for their future success*'.

However, 'cultural capital' and its original roots can be found in the work of the sociologist Bourdieu (1984), who was concerned with the inequality present in society, the head start that this may give some over others and how this may influence educational outcomes and prospects. Fundamentally, Bourdieu (1984) believed every individual possesses 'cultural capital'. Examples can be seen in the way a person speaks, their hobbies and interests etc, which are a product of their socio-cultural background. A key facet of Bourdieu's 'cultural capital' is that society places higher value on certain aspects of capital. Therefore, 'cultural capital' is a complicated concept that from an EYT's perspective is concerned with giving children the best possible start to their early education regardless of background or prior experiences. As an ECT it is imperative to recognise this to effectively assess and provide authentic learning experiences that will support all learners to progress (Bradbury, 2013). Critically, Brodie and Savage (2015, p 21) argue that although it is widely acknowledged that all children are different, there is still a tendency to use language that intonates they tread the same '*predictable path of learning and development'* when assessing progress against what is *'typical'* or *'age related'*. Instead, they advocate applying a socio-cultural approach to assessment where each child's unique characteristics and individuality can be valued. For you, as an EYT, this means adopting an approach where the child is actively involved in their learning journey and there is an opportunity to negotiate learning through shared consensus between you and the *unique child*.

This genuine interest in the child's voice, their curiosities, prior experience and trust in their ability to learn will support you to plan, facilitate, assess and review meaningful learning opportunities to develop their unique and individual learning story. Sometimes you will need to be brave and throw caution to the wind because children who are curious will have lots of questions which will take learning down unpredictable tangents that do not always fit with your plan. Nevertheless, research conducted by Dr Prachi Shah, a developmental and behavioural paediatrician (cited in Berliner, 2020), suggests that curious children perform better and that promoting curiosity could have the potential to close the achievement gap. Interestingly, in Shah's study, the children from economically disadvantaged backgrounds had the strongest connection between curiosity and increased performance.

## Reflective task ◀◀◀

- What are the potential factors that may influence the *unique child* beginning their school journey on an unequal footing?

- What impact might these influencing factors have on the *unique child's* learning journey?

- How might you as an ECT better understand a child's prior experiences and background?

- What can you do to nurture the *unique child's* curiosity?

## Top tips ◀◀◀

- Many factors may influence a child such as social, emotional, economic, physical or cultural aspects of their lives, those of their family and the community around them.

- The opportunities that children have may be vastly varied due to the means that their families have at home. An example of this may be seen in the access to books or modelling of reading by an adult, which can have a direct impact on a child's reading success.

- The induction and transition processes that are in place in your setting or school will support you to gain a clearer understanding of the *unique child*. This and the knowledge you gather over time will equip you to support and tailor their learning journey to meet the individual's needs and the pace at which they learn.

- Be interested, inquisitive, patient and understanding. A key characteristic for you as an EYT is empathy – placing yourself in the child's shoes. Every child has the potential to learn, develop and grow, given the time, nurturing and environment.

## Precious stones with potential to shine

The current landscape in the wake of the Covid-19 global pandemic and its disruptive impact on the economy, health and education has sparked much debate in the early years (EY) education sector. The focus on the youngest children who are now entering EY settings and the impact on 'school readiness' due to missed social and developmental opportunities will inevitably be an additional challenge for you as an ECT. Brenner and Mistry (2020) recognise that the effect of the pandemic on early childhood development needs to be a priority for researchers as the world moves forward. Those working in roles across the EY sector have always considered the impact of 'school readiness' for those at the end of the EYFS in Reception settings who are transitioning to Key Stage 1. In this context, children who have achieved a Good Level of Development (GLD) at the end of the EYFS are considered to be *'school ready'* (MacTavish, 2019).

However, many EY practitioners, parents and carers also consider preparation for a child's Reception year in terms of 'school readiness'. There continues to be discourse surrounding a shared consensus and definition of the term 'school ready'. Regardless of this debate, preparing individuals for their next step, whether this be to Reception or Year 1, may be of further challenge to those who are often described as 'vulnerable children' in an educational context. Vulnerable groups in EY include but are not limited to:

» those who have diagnosed or undiagnosed SEND;

» looked after children (LAC);

» Gypsy, Roma and Travellers (GRT);

» asylum seekers, refugees and new migrants;

» summer-born children.

As an example of the impact this can have, consider how summer-born children may be up to 12 months younger than their peers in the same year group. As an EYT, you may need to take account of this since a good deal of learning and development occurs in a single year of a young child's life. Interestingly, throughout the EYFS phase and up until the end of Reception, children are assessed in terms of age-appropriate expectations.

Many EY practitioners use *Development Matters* (DfE, 2021b) to guide good EY pedagogy and practice. Nonetheless, at the end of the Reception year, teachers assess against the standardised Early Learning Goal (ELG) statements regardless of the child's chronological age. Although it cannot always be justified that chronological age is a predeterminer of academic success, some research has demonstrated a direct correlation between summer-born children and later poorer academic achievement when compared to those with Autumn-term birthdays (Long, 2016; Norbury et al, 2016). In agreement, Campbell (2013) highlights that by the time a summer-born child is seven years old, more are in lower-ability groups, particularly those with August birthdays. Contrastingly, Rodger (2012) argues that there is a risk of treating summer-born children as immature compared to their older peers. Consequently, practitioners may be tempted to limit opportunities or lower their expectations, which may be detrimental to a summer-born learners' self-confidence and development.

Mitchell (2019) adds to the summer-born debate, contending that some Reception classes may have a more structured approach to ensure children are *school ready*. This has implications for those children who may need a more play-based approach suited to their developmental needs regardless of their chronological age. Therefore, continuous formative assessment will enable you to know every *unique child* well, supporting you to extend learning as they progress towards the ELGs at the end of their Reception year.

## Reflective task ◀◀◀

- What skills and knowledge do children need to be 'school ready'?

- How can you support children in your setting to be 'school ready'?

- Can you think of any examples of children or groups of learners who may need a more bespoke approach in your current setting? What are their needs and how can you adapt practice to meet their needs?

- Think about the prime areas of learning in the EYFS (DfE, 2021a) to help you to frame your ideas about the skills and knowledge children need to be school ready, eg, personal, social and emotional development:

  - separates from parents/carer;

  - communicates own needs;

  - listens to others;

  - dresses independently;

  - understands behaviour expectations;

  - confident to try new activities;

  - takes turns/shares.

- Steadily introducing the children to new routines may support with 'school readiness', such as joining the school for assemblies, dressing into school PE kit for physical development sessions, joining the school playground at playtimes, having lunch in the school hall etc.

- Some settings adapt their learning environment at key points across the academic year to support the children's next steps. For example, a more formal approach in the Summer term of Reception where the children have longer periods of focused activities, or continuous provision opportunities as they enter the Autumn term in Year 1.

## Unlocking the treasure trove

Hellyn and Bennett (2019), founders of 'The Curiosity Approach', advocate that children are born with innate curiosity and that the well-being and development of young children is being compromised in the ever-evolving digital world. They believe that a learning environment with innovatively created spaces, open-ended and 'loose part' authentic resources play a vital role in inspiring 'awe and wonder' and children's inquisitiveness to explore, investigate and solve problems. As an EYT, promoting curiosity primed opportunities while ensuring progress for every child can be a challenging balance to manage. For some children their ideal learning environment may be outdoors, where they can explore in less contained spaces, out in the fresh air. It can be surprising how children who appear reticent or lack motivation in the indoor classroom can shine and become natural leaders of their own and others' learning and play when exposed to an environment conducive to their needs.

Early childhood pioneers including Froebel (cited in Bruce, 2012) and McMillan (cited in Bradburn, 1976) have long advocated and emphasised the importance of outdoor play and learning. The world over, EY educators incorporate outdoor learning experiences into their curriculum and for some, the outdoors is at the beating heart of the enabling earning environment. Forest School, inspired by Scandinavian EY practice (Knight, 2013), has developed significantly in UK EY pedagogy over the past few decades. However, the practicalities surrounding adult-to-child ratios and the expense attached to training new Forest School leaders inevitably falls to schools with already stretched budgets. Still, this should not deter you from providing high-quality outdoor learning opportunities. With creativity and shrewd resourcing, as described in the previous chapter, you will be able to transform even the most limited outdoor space into an area that ignites *awe and wonder* in the children. The element of choice is often another area that can pose contentions for even the most experienced EYT. How much choice and autonomy do the children have and how will you ensure that a balance of experience, skills development and learning is evidenced across the EYFS or Key Stage 1 curriculum?

Some children will need more scaffolding and direction, whereas others may be adept at leading their own learning. There will always be those children who gravitate towards the construction area or sand tray and can rarely be persuaded to visit the writing table. Relatively new to the repertoire of EY pedagogical practice is the concept of the 'Rainbow Challenge', which can support the transition to Year 1 and the learning that follows (Wellborne, 2019).

The principle of this approach is that the children are motivated to collect seven colours (eg ribbons, lollypop sticks, counters, pegs) throughout the week. A colour is assigned to learning challenges across the seven EYFS areas of development or Key Stage 1 curriculum (eg mathematical, writing, creative, construction or problem-solving challenges). This enables you as the teacher to carefully plan weekly challenges that ensure a range of skills are developed across the broad and balanced curriculum while enticing children to visit and complete challenges, adding the corresponding activity colour to their own personal rainbow. Bottrill (2020, p 58) contends that the essence of any well-designed continuous provision should not be overcomplicated and can be simplified to the three Ms – *'Making conversation, mark making and mathematics'*. These fundamental skills are central to preparing children for their future world and can be applied to reading, writing, measuring, counting etc with *'making conversation'*, through extending children's vocabulary and engaging them in a talk-rich environment, an overarching feature of any experience they encounter.

Your role as an EYT is to plan for this dialogue by arming yourself with vocabulary, questions and purposeful chatter to extend and enhance the children's knowledge and understanding. Of equal importance are your skills as a listener, which will support you to engage children in two-way meaningful conversations. Bottrill (2020, p 61) goes on to describe the secretly hidden but equally important three Ms, suggesting these are not always valued by adults as children progress in their schooling:

1. muscle and movement;

2. mindfulness;

3. magic.

In many ways these may happen incidentally through the experiences that you facilitate for the children, but they are by no means of lesser importance.

## Reflective task ◀◀◀

- How will you ignite curiosity, awe and wonder for the children that you teach?

- If teaching in Year 1, how will you support the transition for those children through continuous provision opportunities?

- How might you develop the 'Rainbow Challenge' or continuous provision as children progress through Year 1?

- What daily or weekly opportunities are available in your classroom to ensure that the children develop in the *three Ms* – 'Making conversation, mark making and mathematics' as well as the secretly hidden *three Ms* – 'Muscle and movement, mindfulness and magic'?

## Top tips ◀◀◀

- Creative hooks are a fantastic way to spark and ignite interest and intrigue for the children. Ideas may include changing the learning environment in some way, music, books, film, intriguing objects etc.

- Have conversations with the teachers/practitioners in the children's previous setting. What can they tell you about the group or individuals' 'Characteristics of Effective Teaching and Learning' and how this knowledge contributed to the continuous provision opportunities? This information can be invaluable to inform discussions as a team about planning, developing practice and learning opportunities that support children's engagement and next steps.

- Consider how planned opportunities in the continuous provision can support, enhance and develop children's knowledge and skills in areas of the Year 1 curriculum. An example of this would be providing children with a role play area where they act as jungle guides, sharing their expert knowledge of species of plants or animals learnt in their science sequence of learning.

- When planning your continuous provision across the week, consider how the activities you provide support children with Bottrill's (2020) three Ms. You could add a code to your plan to clarify where the three Ms and the further 'secret' three Ms occur, eg, mark making (MM), mathematics (M), making conversation (MC), muscles and movement (M&M), mindfulness (MF) and magic (MG).

# So what?

## What difference does it make?

## Reflective task ◀◀◀

Gaining insight into the record keeping and assessment procedures in your school setting will help you to better understand how you can support pupil progress over time and contribute to pupil progress meetings. Such meetings may take place weekly as part of your phase team or as a whole school, dependent on the size of the team. These meetings are vital to ensure that individuals and groups of children are identified and supported through intervention in a timely manner. Review what is currently used in your setting to track progress and how the team uses this information to inform practice to ensure children continue to progress.

Does the tracking system and professional dialogue used in progress meetings show a consideration for the following?

- Baseline data (RBA) or informal initial assessments (Key Stage 1/2 teacher assessments).

- Evidence of a child's holistic journey over time (learning journeys, evidence in books, anecdotal evidence, contributions from parents/carers and other professionals).

- Development and progress which is age related or age expected (eg *Development Matters*, DfE, 2021b is frequently used in EY) or indicates if children are working at *expected* level against the Key Stage 1 national curriculum descriptors.

- EYFSP data – standardised benchmark of '*emerging*' or '*expected*' for each ELG.

- GLD for individual children.

- Recognition at the end of EYFS that individuals may be '*emerging*' due to their personal journey, progress and developmental journey.

- Transition procedures at the end of EYFS or the next year group.

- Records of interventions for individuals and groups of learners with reviews that inform next steps or future interventions.

- Individuals recognised as needing stretch and challenge to ensure substantial progress is maintained.

## Case study ◀◀◀

The case study shown in Table 5.1 tracks the progress of a child throughout the EYFS from a pre-school setting into Reception and as Child A transitions to Year 1. The teacher records key conversations with parents; progress tracking; recommendations for parents/carers; key interventions at school; the impact of interventions; and data benchmarks against *Development Matters* (DfE, 2021b) at key points throughout the academic year. These planned interventions are additional to the '*quality first teaching*' that Child A receives throughout the academic year. By the end of Child A's Reception year, EYFS profile data against the Early Learning Goals (DfE, 2021a) identifies that this child has not reached a GLD and looks at recommendations moving forward into Year 1. The intention of this case study is to support you to identify how tracking learning, development and progress over time is used to support the individual child and how early and strategic intervention is a key indicator of learner progress.

**Table 5.1 Progress and intervention case study**

| Key information – Child A | Medical: | Pre-school experience: |
|---|---|---|
| **Date of birth:** 01-06-17 (summer birthday) | • Inhaler for asthma | • Childminder setting, 5 days |
| **Family background:** Only child | • Breathing difficulties – early infancy | • 10 sessions – on-site pre-school (Summer term) |
| **AUTUMN TERM** | **SPRING TERM** | **SUMMER TERM** |
| **September – Initial teacher observations:** | **January – Progress review with parent/ carer:** | **April – Interim EYFS Profile judgements:** |
| • Good gross motor skills; enjoys outdoor learning/PE | • Continued difficulties focusing during phonics | • ELG 'expected' – S, GMS, BR, SR, MS |
| • Plays alone; little communication with peers | • Support with phonics – take home resource pack | • ELG 'emerging' – LAU, WR, C, W, N, NP, FMS |
| • Difficulty following instructions | **Home support recommendations:** | **Home support recommendations:** |
| • Strong focus – chosen play activities | • Parent to see GP – eyes/ears check-up | • Parent invited to after-school maths club |
| **Teacher observations/RBA data:** | • Parent invited to after-school phonics club | • Number recognition games, phonics/ reading activities |
| **SBT** – LAU, S, SR, BR | **Planned school interventions:** | **Planned school interventions:** |
| **BT** – MS, WR, C, W, FMS, N, NP | • 'Phonics and Cookies' club (2 × week – teacher) | • 'Maths Munchers' club (2 × week – teacher) |
| **T** – GMS | | • Phase 3 phonemes/tricky words (3 × week – TA) |

**October – Parent/carer consultation:**
- Strength in gross motor – loves football/outdoors
- Settling in/securing friendships in the group
- Fine motor control difficulties, gross motor strength
- Challenges in focusing attention – activities/carpet time

**Home support recommendations:**
- Fine motor activities, eg modelling dough/scissors/threading
- Adult modelling reading

**Planned school interventions:**
- Extra-curricular 'Yoga Tots' and 'Squiggle and Wiggle' clubs 1 (2 × week – teacher)

- Phonics to secure phase 2/3 phonemes (daily – teacher)
- Maths – number (3 × week – TA)
- 'Time to talk' (3 × week – TA)

**March – Parent/carer consultation:**
- Developing relationships with peers; still physical at times
- Increased confidence/built good relationships with adults

**Home support recommendations:**
- Number recognition games
- Phonics/reading activities
- Eyes/ears checked – all fine

- Maths – number patterns (3 × week – TA)

**June – End of EYFSP data:**

**ELG 'expected'** – LAU, S, FMS, GMS, N, BR, SR, MS

**ELG 'emerging'** – C, WR, W, NP
- GLD not achieved
- Good progress made from 'BT' and some 'SBT' age-related expectation starting points

**July – Parent/carer consultation – Year 1 transition:**
- Reception, Year 1 teacher, SENDCo met with parent/carer to discuss transition/next steps

| | Planned school interventions: | • End-of-year report shared/discussed – highlighted areas for development in listening, attention and understanding, maths, writing, reading. |
|---|---|---|
| • Initial sounds/CV/CVC word building 1:1 (daily – TA) | • Strategies – carpet time focus | |
| • Time to talk (3 × week – TA) | • Additional small group phonics (3 × week – TA) | **Planned Year 1 interventions:** |
| **December – Impact of interventions:** | • Writing/fine motor intervention group (daily – TA) | • Daily reading – rehearse phonics/word building |
| • Increased confidence to share ideas with peers/adults | **March – Impact of interventions:** | • Lego 'talk' club |
| • Recognising some Phase 2 phonemes | • Increased confidence in speaking/focus in groups | • Number patterns – to 20 |
| • Can segment CV, CVC words; unable to blend | • Retaining Phase 2, some Phase 3 phonemes/blending | • Sentence writing – applying tricky words/phonics |
| **End of Autumn term data:** | • Blending words – adult modelled | |
| **SBT** – LAU, S, SR, | • Recognising numbers to 10 | |
| **BT** – BR, S, MS, WR, C, W, FMS, NP, | **End of Spring term data:** | |
| **T** – GMS | **BT** – LAU, S, C, WR, W, FMS, N, NP | |
| | **T** – GMS, BR, SR, MS | |

**Table 5.2 Key of abbreviations**

| EYFS – Early Years Foundation Stage<br><br>ELG – Early Learning Goals<br><br>RBA – Reception Baseline Assessment<br><br>SBT – Significantly below age-related expectations<br><br>BT – Below typical age-related expectations<br><br>T – Typical age-related expectations | **Prime area: Personal, Social and Emotional Development**<br><br>SR – Self-regulation<br><br>MS – Managing self<br><br>BR – Building relationships | **Prime area:**<br><br>**Physical Development**<br><br>GMS – Gross motor skills<br><br>FMS – Fine motor skills<br><br>**Communication and Language**<br><br>LAU – Listening, attention and understanding<br><br>S – Speaking | **Specific area: Literacy**<br><br>C – Comprehension<br><br>WR – Word reading<br><br>W – Writing<br><br>**Mathematics**<br><br>N – Number<br><br>NP – Number patterns |
|---|---|---|---|

## Reflective task ◀◀◀

Using the case study provided for Child A in Table 5.1, reflect upon the impact of strategic and timely interventions and the cycle of 'Assess, Plan, Do, Review' referred to in the SEND Code of Practice (DfE, 2015, pp 86–7). The questions below will support you to consider how you will approach interventions that will support pupil progress in your own practice.

- How did strategic interventions support Child A to progress?

- Which areas did Child A progress in over the course of the Reception year?

- How did the teacher involve parents/carers in the child's learning journey?

- Which interventions appeared to have the most impact on Child A's progress?

- Are there any further interventions that you could suggest to improve the support and progress for Child A in their Reception year?

- What interventions will support Child A to progress in Year 1?

# Now what? ◀◀◀

## Practical ways to implement this in the classroom

## Practical task for tomorrow ◀◀◀

Look carefully at where your children are, not only by using the RBA, if entering Reception, but also your own observations of children entering the EY setting, including any transition information from previous settings and interactions with parents/carers. If you are teaching children in Key Stage 1, EYFSP data will be useful to ascertain whether individuals have reached their GLD. Conversations with the EY team will be vital in supporting you to fully understand the individual's 'Characteristics of Effective Learning' and their progress over the course of the Foundation Stage. Consider how well you know the children, particularly those in your class who could potentially slip under your radar. Often these children are the quieter participators within the group who always sit and demonstrate desired learning behaviours. Carve out time in your week to have one-to-one interactions and converse with these children to build that vital rapport and understand a little more about them.

## Practical task for next week ◀◀◀

Begin to have vital conversations with the EY lead and Key Stage 1 lead surrounding assessment and tracking pupil progress, as well as assessment procedures pertinent to the year group you are teaching. Often schools have their own tracking system and these may differ from school to school. Having an overview of the key points across the academic year when tracking systems are updated and the evidence that contributes to this will support you to have a bigger picture of how formative assessment supports summative judgements over time. Equally, understanding how the school identifies individuals and groups of children who need strategic intervention and those pupils who need to be challenged and stretched can assist you to have an impact on teaching and learning, ensuring that every child reaches their full potential.

## Practical task for the long term ◀◀◀

As you approach the Spring/Summer term, inevitably you will be compiling end-of-year reports. Keeping anecdotal notes, annotated examples of work and records such as learning journeys can really help you to be more efficient in the summative report writing process. It can be difficult to remember how children got on with projects or learning in the Autumn term; therefore, keeping a running record of comments that you would like to add to written reports may save you a good deal of time overall. Your summative commentary about children's progress will frame discussions with colleagues that your children will be transitioning to in the upcoming academic year. Transitional conversations may include the child's new teacher, the SENDCo and the parent/carer, particularly if there is concern with areas of learning, behaviour and diagnosed or undiagnosed SEND. As a teacher receiving a new child to your class, these meetings will help you to understand ways in which you can support a smoother transition for the child, as well as share information about the individuals who may need interventions either socially or academically in preparation.

# What next?

## Further reading

Bottrill, G (2020) *School and the Magic of Children*. London: Sage.

Palaiologou, I (2019) *Child Observation: A Guide for Students of Early Childhood*. 4th ed. London: Sage.

Reardon, D, Wilson, D and Fox Reed, D (2018) *Early Years Teaching and Learning*. 3rd ed. Los Angeles: Sage.

## References

Berliner, W (2020) How Curiosity is Key to Learning. [online] Available at: www.earlyye arseducator.co.uk/features/article/focus-how-curiosity-is-key-to-learning (accessed 13 August 2022).

Bottrill, G (2020) *School and the Magic of Children*. London: Sage.

Bourdieu, P (1984) *Distinction: A Social Critique of the Judgement of Taste*. Cambridge, MA: Harvard University Press.

Bradburn, E (1976) *Margaret McMillan: Framework and Expansion of Nursery Education*. Nutfield, Surrey: Denholm House Press.

Bradbury, A (2013) *Understanding Early Years Inequality*. Abingdon: Routledge.

Brenner, A and Mistry, S (2020) Child Development During the COVID-19 Pandemic Through a Life Course Theory Lens. *Child Development Perspectives*, 14(4): 236–43.

Brodie, K and Savage, K (2015) *Inclusion and Early Years Practice*. Abingdon: Routledge.

Bruce, E (2012) *Early Childhood Practice: Froebel Today*. London: Sage.

Campbell, T (2013) *In-school Ability Grouping and the Month of Birth Effect: Preliminary Evidence from the Millennium Cohort Study*. London: Institute of Education, London University.

Department for Education (DfE) (2015) *Special Educational Needs and Disability Code of Practice: 0 to 25 Years*. London: Crown.

Department for Education (DfE) (2021a) *Statutory Framework for the Early Years Foundation Stage*. London: Department for Education.

Department for Education (DfE) (2021b) *Development Matters: Non-statutory Curriculum Guidance for the Early Years Foundation Stage*. London: Crown.

Hellyn, L and Bennett, S (2019) *From Ordinary to Extraordinary*. Great Britain: The Curiosity Approach.

Knight, S (2013) *Forest School and Outdoor Learning in the Early Years*. London: Sage.

Long, R (2016) *Summer-Born Children Starting School*. House of Commons Library Briefing Paper No. 07272.

MacBlain, S (2022) *Learning Theories for Early Years Practice*. 2nd ed. London: Sage.

MacTavish, A (2019) Ready or Not? [online] Available at: https://eyfs.info/articles.html/personal-social-and-emotional-development/ready-or-not-r257 (accessed 13 August 2022).

Mitchell, E (2019) A Small-scale Exploratory Study of Educator's Perceptions and Expectations of Summer-born Children in the Reception Classes of Three English Primary Academies and the Strategies Used to Support Them. *Education 3–13*, 47: 205–16.

Norbury, C F, Gooch, D, Baird, G, Charman, T, Simonoff, E and Pickles, A (2016) Younger Children Experience Lower Levels of Language Competence and Academic Progress in the First Year of School: Evidence from a Population Study. *Journal of Child Psychology and Psychiatry*, 57: 65–73.

Ofsted (2019) *Early Years Inspection Handbook*. London: Crown.

Rodger, R (2012) *Planning an Appropriate Curriculum in the Early Years*. 3rd ed. Abingdon: Routledge.

Standards and Testing Agency (2021) *Reception Baseline Assessment and Reporting Arrangements*. London: Crown.

Wellbourne, V (2019) Placing Well – Being at the Heart of Year 1 Pedagogy. [online] Available at: www.earlyyearseducator.co.uk/features/article/placing-well-being-at-the-heart-of-year-1-pedagogy (accessed 13 August 2022).

# Chapter 6    Ongoing development as an early years professional

## What? (The big idea)

### Taking ownership of your professional journey

As an early career teacher (ECT), you will find yourself on a professional learning journey and you will be growing in confidence and competence as an early years teacher (EYT). As research such as Smith (2007) indicates, this will involve you acquiring differing types of knowledge, ie pedagogical and subject matter knowledge and subject-specific pedagogic knowledge. Linked to such accumulation of knowledge, which is tangible to you and your practice, you will also be continuing to develop your sense of professional identity (a notion explored in Chapter 1). As researchers agree (Beijaard et al, 2004; Lasky, 2005) a teacher's identity is dynamic in its nature and will shift as they continue to professionally grow. Such professional development will not only aid the construction of their professional identity but, as Avidov-Ungar (2016, p 665) outlines, it 'helps determine the type of professional path they follow'.

As you progress through your ECT years you will continue to consider who you are as a teacher. You will also think about how you see your career developing regarding your future roles and responsibilities in the profession. This may take the form of a nagging question, 'What do I want to do next in my career?' You will not be alone in such a feeling; remember these thoughts are quite natural. As you progress, these future roles and responsibilities will manifest themselves into what is often referred to as a career trajectory. However, research such as Brunetti and Marston (2018) indicates that such career development can often be shaped by many factors, including the school context (and its internal factors) and external circumstances (eg a teacher's personal life). Your career trajectory will also be underpinned by your motivations and aspirations for your future. These will continue to evolve and change. As Hirsh and Bergmo-Prvulovic (2019, p 368) indicate when considering the idea of a career, it is 'better understood as a continuous process of exchange rather than a destination'. Rather than being seen as climbing a ladder, it involves a continuous construction of knowledge, which itself is growing in its difficulty of challenge (Hirsh and Bermo-Prvulovic, 2019).

Whatever your professional future ambitions are, it will involve the sharing of your professional knowledge. This may be among your colleagues in school, other settings or in a leadership role. It will also involve using the many wonderful transferable skills you will have acquired as an EY ECT, such as being an effective communicator. You will also not be alone when developing your future goals. Relationships with your mentor and your setting's leadership team will also enable and support you in your future career development.

As an emerging, highly skilled practitioner, this chapter considers:

» what it is you can offer to the profession as you contemplate your future goals;

» the importance of others in supporting the shaping of your future career;

» the need for taking ownership of your EY professional journey so that it can be moulded to what you desire it to be;

» how ambition can play a role in moulding your future career aspirations.


## What might your future hold?

Moving towards the successful completion of your ECT period, you will no doubt be encouraged to look forward to future career opportunities. These will both complement and utilise your EY knowledge and expertise. Research such as Day et al (2007, p 69) suggests that teachers' professional development may be seen in what they deem as *'professional life phases'*. This research suggests that an individual's professional development may happen in what Day et al (2007, p 82) consider to be the watershed period of teaching (professional life phase, 8–15 years). In this period, individuals go on to progress in their future professional careers. However, all teachers are different; you will know when the time is right for you to seek further professional developmental opportunities, roles and responsibilities.

It is also important to say that individuals will all have different reasons to take on any such new challenges. For Hirsh and Bergmo-Prvulovic (2019, pp 366–7) it may be for one of the following *'stances'*: an altruist stance (mainly to do good for others), a reciprocal stance (doing good for oneself and others along with external rewards) or an individualist stance (an individual agenda of salary and status). Though, as they note, these *'stances'* should not be seen as static; they can vary over time (due to circumstance) and an individual can adopt more or less of each of these *'stances'* over time.

A key message with regard to any further professional development is that you should find a future that suits you. For some teachers that may mean remaining in the classroom and mainly undertaking class teaching. For others, they will take on leadership roles within or outside their setting. These may include co-ordinating a subject or mentoring a trainee teacher. Taking on such roles may ultimately lead you on to becoming a phase leader or becoming an assistant head or headteacher. Whatever the role, you should find the level that suits you and what you wish to be demanded of yourself. It is important also to remember how you will sustain that all-important work–life balance too when considering the demands of any future role.

## What can you offer to any future role?

As an EYT, you will have developed many transferrable skills and qualities, some learned and built through experience. These will be vital for your future career and the roles and responsibilities you wish to take on. Table 6.1 outlines some of these vital skills you no doubt will have developed. Also included are some examples of how these skills may be seen in your daily practice.

**Table 6.1 Valuable skills**

| Skill | How it may manifest itself |
|---|---|
| **Effective communicator** | *Examples*<br><br>• Helping children to form and develop their speech in your class.<br><br>• Dealing with and informing parents regarding their child's progress. |
| **Organised** | *Examples*<br><br>• Resourcing, researching and planning for the many different activities in your classroom.<br><br>• Keeping on top of your formative assessments and using software such as Tapestry will help inform parents of their child's progress. |
| **Able to build relationships** | *Examples*<br><br>• Given your children's young developmental age, showing empathy will help them effectively deal with and self-regulate their evolving emotions.<br><br>• Listening to parents and carers will help you build effective relationships. |
| **Adaptable** | *Examples*<br><br>• There are many times when things do not go as predicted with younger children so you will have to think on your feet.<br><br>• When children are struggling with a new daunting experience, for example singing in the nativity, you will have to quickly find other means to achieve your goals for them. |
| **Creativity** | *Examples*<br><br>• You will have had to find fun and creative ways of engaging children in learning.<br><br>• Develop creative activities which will engage pupils' fine motor skills, thus boosting their literacy and cognitive skills. |

Your skills and attitudes will form part of a personal toolkit which will be invaluable in your future professional goals, for example, when dealing with moderators of your early years (EY) baselines and Early Years Foundation Stage (EYFS) profile data or, even further into your future career, perhaps mentoring a trainee teacher. For such roles, you will need to be able to quickly build effective relationships with these individuals. You will need to be approachable and be able to use effective interpersonal skills. These may include communication, empathy and trust.

## Reflective task ◀◀◀

- Using Table 6.2 think about your own personal skills and attitudes toolkit.

- As well as considering what others may say about you professionally, think about what skills and qualities you have and utilise in your day-to-day teaching and when managing the children and adults in your setting. How can these enhance any future roles and responsibilities you wish to achieve? Are some better developed than others?

- Now rank these traits in order from areas of strength to areas of development.

- Reflect on whether there is anything you can do to enhance your current levels of skill to make them of greater value to you in the future.

**Table 6.2 Personal skills**

| Ranking | Skills | Qualities | Considered enhancements |
|---------|--------|-----------|-------------------------|
| Area of development ↕ strength | | | |

## Who and what may help with career guidance?

Given the ongoing professional relationship you will have developed with your mentor, they may be the first person you wish to talk to with regard to your thoughts about your future goals. Mentors are good listeners; someone you trust and who can show empathy (Howard et al, 2020), and as such they will prove a good sounding board for how you feel you would like your career to progress. Like other colleagues in your school, they too will have learnt what a career trajectory can look like, entail and how it can be achieved. Initial opportunities for you to take on future responsibilities may have already come up. This includes, for example, leading staff meetings for knowledge exchange and partnership with colleagues in other settings. Seize these opportunities since they will help to build your confidence and skill sets. As time goes on, other roles will inevitably come your way such as a subject co-ordinator. To enhance your skills and knowledge you may wish to start to consider additional forms of professional development to enhance your suitability for future career roles. As Spencer et al (2018, p 42) note, for ECTs, professional development may be seen as something 'essentially concerned with preparation, for the next stage of their teaching career, including managing others'. To these ends, professional development may not only serve to enhance your knowledge, skills (or both) but also can relate to a role in future school management or an enhanced educational focus. One example of professional development that might enhance your knowledge, skills and behaviours and qualification for future leadership is the NPQ for Early Years Leadership (DfE, 2021). This course has been designed to support the professional development of teachers (as well as school leaders) in school settings. Other professional development opportunities linked to enhancing your suitability and qualifications might include a Postgraduate Certificate in Education (PGCE), Masters of Education (MEd) or Masters of Arts (MA). These courses can be taken via face-to-face tuition or online.

## Reflective task ◀◀◀

Use Table 6.3 or create your own to audit your achievements as you progress through your initial period of teaching. This will serve as a means to record what you have to offer any setting as your future career develops and will help you identify where you have made significant progress in supporting your setting and where you can enhance your professional development.

**Table 6.3 Professional audit**

| Timescale | Role/experience | Enhancements in training or qualification |
|---|---|---|
| ECT Year 1 | *Example. Running an after-school club.* | *Risk assessment training.* |
| ECT Year 2 | *Example. Moderating baseline assessment as part of an audit.* | *Half-day training with your local EY cluster to prepare for the audit.* |

## Top tips ◀◀◀

- Update your CPD record when it happens. It can be easy to forget what a course that you attended covered and the impact it had on your practice.

- Reflect upon these training events and get into the habit of recording what you will do this week, next week and in the future as a result. It can also be useful to consider who you will need to liaise with and what resources are needed to meet these objectives.

- Keep a log of your contributions to the team and school throughout your ECT journey; these can act as useful reminders of the breadth of your role and experience.

# So what? ◀ ◀ ◀

## What difference does it make?

As an early years teacher (EYT), you can often feel 'pigeonholed' or categorised by what is a perceived identity by others of what you are like given your work in this key phase. Given the EYFS curricular framework some may overlook the depth and breadth of your subject knowledge. They may also underestimate your skills and attitudes due to the urban myth that all you do in EY is play! Remember, however, the important factor is who you feel you are, ie your unique professional identity. Linked to your current identity is also the idea of who you want to be professionally. These two parts of your identity form part of what Evans (1998, p 24) might deem the 'real self' and the 'ideal self'. It is the 'ideal self' that will mould and drive your future goals, motivations and aspirations in your career.

There will be many drivers for who you wish to be and it is important you reflect upon what motivates and inspires you in your future. Such an honest reflection of such factors is vital if you are to follow the best route to achieve your professional future self in your future career.

Research by Avidov-Ungar (2016) can provide a useful framework for such reflection. It not only serves to demonstrate the dynamic nature of an individual's professional development but also provides a four-pattern typology for professional development. This is in terms of an *'individual's motivations (intrinsic or extrinsic) and aspirations (lateral or vertical)'* (Avidov-Ungar, 2016, p 662). Figure 6.1 summarises and outlines Avidov-Ungar's (2016) findings regarding the four patterns of professional development.

| | | The motivation that underpins professional development | |
|---|---|---|---|
| | | Intrinsic | Extrinsic |
| The aspirations which underpin professional development | Vertical | **Hierarchically ambitious** *Example. A person who has a personal desire from within to progress managerially.* | **Hierarchically compelled** *Example. A person with a desire and commitment to move forward managerially and is driven by gaining some responsibility.* |
| | Lateral | **Laterally ambitious** *Example. A person who has a desire to develop their professional skills at classroom level and does not wish to progress managerially.* | **Laterally compelled** *Example. A person who wishes and is obligated to know more and to develop their professional skills at classroom level and is monetarily driven.* |

**Figure 6.1 A model of teachers' perceptions of professional development including an integration of example-subsumed case descriptors, derived from research by Avidov-Ungar (2016)**

As an EYT, you must not underestimate the number of many transferrable skills and attitudes you have to offer the profession in whatever future role you undertake.

## Reflective task ◀◀◀

Consider the many other professionals that you have met in your school and network who have supported your journey so far.

- Are any of these roles something that you would like to do?

- List those factors that might motivate you in the future to take on any additional responsibilities.

- Use Table 6.4 or create your own to map your reflections on the future drivers for your future professional career.

**Table 6.4 Progression audit**

| One year after ECT has ended | | Five years | | Ten years | |
|---|---|---|---|---|---|
| **Role or responsibility** | **Motivator** | **Role or responsibility** | **Motivator** | **Role or responsibility** | **Motivator** |
| *Example* | *Example* | *Example* | *Example* | *Example* | *Example* |
| Art co-ordinator | Enjoy teaching the subject | Phase leader | Wishing to become assistant head | Assistant headteacher | Enhanced salary and pension |

## Case study ◀◀◀

### Milana

Milana has just finished her time as an ECT. She works in a three-form entry school teaching in Reception. Milana has started to want to have some more leadership experience and ultimately wishes to become a phase leader. To aid this journey she has begun to reflect on the value of further study.

*I never thought that I would like to go back to university to study but now I have had a few years of teaching experience I have started to realise how much I still have to learn about children, their development, my pedagogy and practice. I know some peers who have done further study and they found it beneficial to them and* their career. By studying at Master of Arts (MA) level, I have heard that it will give me the opportunity to broaden my educational focus beyond that of my class and school. Having researched several courses, I realised I was able to learn about items such as international perspectives on early years. Other modules seemed to focus on policy and contemporary issues that would mould us as future practitioners. I realised that my study would bring me into contact again with research relating to young children's learning, the curriculum and practice in early childhood education. I looked forward to becoming a researcher again and finding out about many focuses relating to early years. My plan was after a few years of extra experience to take on a co-ordination role. Then with a completed masters, I would be in the best position possible to apply for a phase leader post.

As a result of the course, Milana had a much-needed opportunity to learn about her practice outside of her setting. This meant she also had the opportunity to talk, learn and network with her peers. She found the course and being with other peers enhanced her own self-reflections and knowledge regards EY policy and practice. Networking with her peers allowed Milana to discuss what she wanted to do in the future professionally while extending her contacts with other settings. Milana's motivation and confidence grew with the course. This newfound confidence and knowledge meant she could present and disseminate her knowledge to other EY co-ordinators to keep them abreast of EY policy, research, pedagogy and practice. This knowledge exchange and MA meant she could enhance her own curriculum vitae (CV) when applying for her identified promotion.

## Reflective task ◀◀◀

- What triggered Milana to engage with professional development?

- Who could Milana talk to with regard to her planned route of study?

- Why did Milana choose this route?

- What were the benefits to Milana's pedagogy, practice and future career aspirations as a result of this professional development?

## Case study ◀◀◀

### Ella's career story

Understanding how young children learn has always been a passion and I specialised in early years in my undergraduate initial teacher training. In the first two years of my career, I taught in Key Stage 1 before securing a role in a single-form entry school as a Reception teacher – my dream job! In this role I was given the freedom and autonomy to make decisions within the setting about early years pedagogy and practice based on my own values and philosophy. This was a big responsibility very early in my career and so I read insatiably about early years management, policy and guidance. Staying abreast of early years practice became a lifelong habit that I still do to this day. I also went about building connections with other early years teachers and practitioners in the local cluster group. In the background, my personal life was changing and I had a young family of my own and a job-share with a super colleague who shared my passion and philosophy. This close collaboration gave rise to opportunities to develop early years practice further – a critical friend that challenged my thinking and took it to the next level. During this time in my career, a visionary headteacher at the school saw the opportunity to open an on-site pre-school. To be a part of the journey from early conception to welcoming the pre-school team and then the first children and parents was both challenging and exciting. This led to an amazing career opportunity when I was asked to be the early years phase leader. Leading an early years team enabled me to collaborate, plan for and disseminate good practice, which contributed to excellent outcomes for the children in our early years setting.

## Reflective task ◀◀◀

- What opportunities did Ella take on her journey?

- Who else was involved in Ella's career progression?

- What did Ella do to support her own development?

- How did Ella balance her personal and career goals?

- Where do you think Ella's career might go next?

- Thinking about your own future professional career goals and development, consider the value of professional development to you. How might obtaining further experience and/or qualifications impact you both personally and professionally? Use the prompts below to aid your reflections.

## Prompts

### How can professional development support my future goals?

- **Top tip:** By continually reflecting on your current practice and considering where you want to be in one, three and five years' time, this will help you to decide when and where professional development is needed and what is appropriate.

### How can I choose the best course to support my future goals?

- **Top tip:** Speak to your mentor and your peers about what courses they have attended. Start looking at a professional course, for example, MA degrees or National Professional Qualifications (NPQs) and the modules they offer. Visit university open days or speak with your local Teaching School Hub; speak to course alumni and tutors who have inside knowledge of the suitability of a course.

### What is the support can my peers offer?

- **Top tip:** By visiting other settings (eg nurseries, early years centres), talking to your peers and getting involved with networks (eg EY co-ordinators), you will hear and see what other opportunities there are for you. You will also have a bank of professionals to turn to when career advice is needed.

# Now what?

## Looking forward

As you continue your professional journey after being an ECT, your professional development will see you taking on many enhanced roles and responsibilities in school and beyond. This will be driven by many factors both intrinsic and extrinsic to yourself. As your career develops you will also see your identity as a teaching professional continue to evolve and drive you on your future path. Your future will see you grow in terms of your knowledge, skills and attitudes towards teaching and this will be nourished by further learning in terms of professional courses. You will not be alone in your future career trajectory; all your peers, some found in teaching networks, will be there to give you help, advice and encouragement. By continually reflecting on that notion of your 'ideal self' you continue to strive for excellence in all you do in your future. All of the above will no doubt leave you at the end of your career feeling professionally fulfilled and be able to look back and wonder '*how did I achieve all of this?*'

## Practical ways to implement this in the classroom

### Practical task for tomorrow

Take time to talk to your mentor about your future professional goals, development and career trajectory. They will know you well and your strong relationship in terms of them being a 'professional critical friend' may mean they are open to such a request. Following this conversation write a 'to-do' list to achieve what was discussed and identified, outlining what you hope for your future career. By checking these off in the future you will achieve a real of sense of achievement over time.

## Practical task for next week ◄◄◄

Keep a log of the skills you use and the roles you take on in your class and the school. The roles you have undertaken, as well as your many skills and qualities, can prove a useful starting point for your own reflections regarding your future goals and targets. These thoughts can inform an audit of your own strengths and areas of development with such insights feeding into your developmental future goals.

## Practical task for the long term ◄◄◄

Consider where you would like to be at the end of your ECT period, in five and ten years' time from now. Talk to colleagues and professional networks about how they achieved these goals and ask them for advice on how you could go about achieving yours. Using Table 6.5 or by making your own table, record your aspirations, the colleagues you could approach and things you might consider doing to achieve your goals.

**Table 6.5 Future aspirations and goals**

|  | End of your ECT | In five years | In ten years |
|---|---|---|---|
| Your goals |  |  |  |
| Who can help and advise you |  |  |  |
| Actions to take |  |  |  |

# What next? ◄ ◄ ◄

## Further reading

Campbell-Barr, V and Leeson, C (2016) *Quality and Leadership in Early Years: Research, Theory and Practice*. London: Sage.

Jones, K and MacPherson, R (2021) *The Teaching Life: Professional Learning and Career Progression*. Woodbridge: John Catt Educational Ltd.

# References

Avidov-Ungar, O (2016) A Model of Professional Development: Teachers' Perceptions of Their Professional Development. *Teachers and Teaching*, 22(6): 653–69.

Beijaard, D, Meijer, P and Verloop, N (2004) Reconsidering Research on Teachers' Professional Identity. *Teaching and Teacher Education*, 20: 107–28.

Brunetti, G J and Marston, S H (2018) A Trajectory of Teacher Development in Early and Mid-career. *Teachers and Teaching*, 24(8): 874–92.

Day, C, Stobart, G, Sammons, P, Kington, A and Qing, G (2007) *Teachers Matter: Connecting Lives, Work and Effectiveness*. London: Open University Press.

Department for Education (DfE) (2021) National Professional Qualification (NPQ): Early Years Leadership Framework. [online] Available at: www.assets.publishing.service.gov.uk/government/uploads/system/uploads/attachment_data/file/1057342/National_Professional_Qualification_for_Early_Years_Leadership.pdf (accessed 13 August 2022).

Evans, L (1998) *Teacher Morale, Job Satisfaction and Motivation*. London: Cassells.

Hirsh, Å and Bergmo-Prvulovic, I (2019) Teachers Leading Teachers – Understanding Middle-leaders' Role and Thoughts about Career in the Context of a Changed Division of Labour. *School Leadership & Management*, 39(3–4): 352–71.

Howard, C, Carroll, J, Owens, J and Langston, D (2020) *The School Mentor's Guide: How to Mentor New and Beginning Teachers*. London. Learning Matters/Sage.

Lasky, S (2005) A Sociocultural Approach to Understanding Teacher Identity, Agency and Professional Vulnerability in a Context of Secondary School Reform. *Teaching and Teacher Education*, 2: 899–916.

Smith, R (2007) Developing Professional Identities and Knowledge: Becoming Primary Teachers. *Teachers and Teaching*, 13(4): 377–97.

Spencer, P, Harrop, S, Thomas, J and Cain, T (2018) The Professional Development Needs of Early Career Teachers, and the Extent to Which They Are Met: A Survey of Teachers in England. *Professional Development in Education*, 44(1): 33–46.

# Acronym buster

| Acronym | What does it stand for? | Notes/links |
|---------|-------------------------|-------------|
| ARA | Assessment and reporting arrangements | |
| BR | Building relationships | |
| BT | Below typical | |
| C | Comprehension | |
| CoETL | Characteristics of Effective Teaching and Learning | |
| CPD | Continuing professional development | |
| CV | Curriculum vitae | |
| DfE | Department for Education | |
| DSL | Designated safeguarding lead | |
| EAL | English as an additional language | |
| ECT | Early career teacher | |
| ELG | Early Learning Goals | |
| EY | Early years | |
| EYE | Early years educator | |
| EYFS | Early Years Foundation Stage | |
| EYFSP | Early Years Foundation Stage Profile | |
| EYT | Early years teacher | |
| FMS | Fine motor skills | |
| GLD | Good level of development | |
| GMS | Gross motor skills | |
| GRT | Gypsy, Roma and Travellers | |
| ITE | Initial teacher education | |
| ITT | Initial teacher training | |
| LAC | Looked after children | |
| LAU | Listening, attention and understanding | |
| MA | Master of Arts | |
| MEd | Master of Education | |
| MKO | More knowledgeable other | |
| MS | Managing self | |
| N | Number | |
| NALDIC | The National Subject Association for EAL | www.naldic.org.uk |

| Acronym | What does it stand for? | Notes/links |
|---|---|---|
| NP | Number patterns | |
| NQP | National Professional Qualification | |
| NRICH | Norwich, (The) Royal Institution, Cambridge (University) and Homerton (College) | www.nrich.maths.org |
| Ofsted | Office for Standards in Education, Children's Services and Skills | |
| PGCE | Postgraduate Certificate in Education | |
| PSED | Personal, social and emotional development | |
| RBA | Reception Baseline Assessment | |
| SBT | Significantly below typical | |
| SEND | Special Educational Needs and Disabilities | |
| SENDCo | Special Educational Needs and Disabilities Co-ordinator | |
| SLT | Senior leadership team | |
| SR | Self-regulation | |
| SST | Sustained shared thinking | |
| TA | Teaching assistant | |
| TED | Teacher education day | |
| W | Writing | |
| WR | Word reading | |

# Index

Note: Page numbers in **bold** and *italics* denote tables and figures, respectively.

Printed in the United States
by Baker & Taylor Publisher Services